SPECTRUM®

Vocabulary

Grade 3

Published by Spectrum®
an imprint of Carson-Dellosa Publishing LLC
Greensboro, NC

Spectrum®
An imprint of Carson-Dellosa Publishing LLC
P.O. Box 35665
Greensboro, NC 27425 USA

ISBN 978-1-4838-1190-1

01-227147811

Table of Contents

Skills Practice

Test-taking Practice

Name _____

Classification is putting objects together in **groups**.
Lemon, **orange**, and **lime** are all **fruits**.
Softball, football, and **soccer** are all **sports**.

Cross out the word in each row that does not belong.

1. golf club   bat   hockey stick   mitt

2. boot   sandal   glove   sneaker

3. necklace   hat   bracelet   earring

4. ankle   thigh   knee   finger

5. lettuce   lemon   carrot   broccoli

6. truck   pogo stick   motorcycle   skateboard

7. window   windshield   toothpick   mirror

8. puppy   doctor   nurse   dentist

9. book   notebook   backpack   workbook

10. toaster   blender   ball bat   refrigerator

Name _____

Find the title in the word box that best names each group of things listed below. Write the title on the line provided.

Sounds	Colors	Vegetables	Cities
Insects	Shapes	Landforms	Feelings

1. _____

carrots, broccoli, peas, beans, asparagus

2. _____

Boston, Dallas, Detroit, Miami, Denver

3. _____

pop, bang, whoosh, crash, splat

4. _____

circle, rectangle, triangle, square, oval

5. _____

purple, tan, maroon, turquoise, yellow

6. _____

lonely, excited, worried, surprised, scared

7. _____

mountains, valleys, hills, plateaus, plains

8. _____

fly, beetle, bee, hornet, ant, moth

Name _____

Cross out the word in each row that does not belong.

1. pine	oak	fir	daisy
2. frog	rock	flower	tree
3. height	weight	eyes	length
4. color	ice	steam	water
5. marker	coupon	pencil	pen
6. blue	yellow	red	black
7. apple	cherry	leaf	banana
8. ant	spider	bee	squirrel
9. stripe	polka dots	pants	plaid
10. viola	drums	cello	violin
11. cloud	rain	thunder	wave
12. river	stream	creek	ocean

Name _____

Use the words from the word box to complete each list of animal homes.

hawk	lion	blue jay
whale	bluebird	robin
polar bear	groundhog	horse
dolphin	tuna	shark

Sky

_____   _____

_____   _____

Sea

_____   _____

_____   _____

Land

_____   _____

_____   _____

Name _____

Look at each group of words below. First cross out the word that does not belong. Then add a word from the word box that does belong.

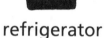					
refrigerator	sweater	fountain	towel	scissors	shovel

1. paper   pencil
    eraser   stapler
    penguin   glue

    _____

2. toothbrush   sausage
    mirror   sink
    soap   washcloth

    _____

3. pans   stove
    dishes   cupboard
    globe   toaster

    _____

4. shirts   soil
    skirts   shoes
    pants   socks

    _____

5. chocolate   hose
    lawnmower   tools
    paint   clippers

    _____

6. swings   benches
    pond   flowers
    grass   pound

    _____

Spectrum Vocabulary Grade 3

Name _____

Synonyms are words that mean the **same** thing.
Big and **huge** are **synonyms**.
Tiny and **small** are **synonyms**.

Circle the two words in each row that mean the same thing.

1.	easy	simple	funny
2.	tiny	baby	small
3.	dance	jump	leap
4.	bumpy	rough	heavy
5.	hear	look	watch
6.	fix	repair	buy
7.	stop	start	begin
8.	quick	fast	run
9.	smile	happy	grin
10.	close	shut	open
11.	fence	home	house
12.	mean	nasty	big

Name _____

Read each sentence. Write a word from the word box that has almost the same meaning as the <u>underlined</u> word.

like	silly	watch	yell	unhappy
fuzzy	largest	turn	scared	leaped

1. I <u>enjoy</u> watching the clowns.   _____

2. The <u>sad</u> clown is the best.   _____

3. He is riding the <u>biggest</u> bike.   _____

4. Watch the bike <u>spin</u> around.   _____

5. Here comes the <u>furry</u> dog.   _____

6. He looks <u>funny</u> in a clown's hat.   _____

7. Did you <u>see</u> the dog jump?   _____

8. It <u>jumped</u> into the basket.   _____

9. Is the dog <u>frightened</u>?   _____

10. Let's clap and <u>shout</u> for the dog! _____

Name _____

Choose a word from the word box that could take the place of the **boldfaced** word in each sentence. Write it on the line provided.

thick	whole	help	choose	careful	piece

1. I will **select** a new tie for Dad.

2. This box is heavy. Will you **assist** me?

3. Today we saw every animal in the **entire** zoo!

4. I'd like a small **portion** of the cake, please.

5. I didn't see you hiding in those **dense** bushes.

6. Be **cautious** when crossing the street.

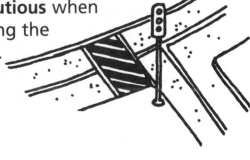

Name _____

Read each sentence. Use the picture clue to help you figure out the meaning of the **boldfaced** word. Circle the correct meaning. Write it on the line.

1. The workers are **constructing** a new house on our street.

_____

building   moving

4. The teacher corrected my spelling **error**.

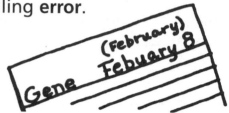

_____

month   mistake

2. Our plane **departed** at ten o'clock.

_____

landed   left

5. Blowing up a balloon **alters** its shape.

_____

changes   colors

3. I waited for Sandy to **reply**.

Dear Sandy,
Can you come to my party on Sunday at 3:00? Let me know.
Your friend,
Keri.

_____

answer   visit

6. He will now **demonstrate** how the robot works.

_____

believe   show

Name _____

Write a synonym for each word using the words from the word box.

tardy	sad	jolly	big	frown	lower	yellow
fat	thin	quiet	lift	close	loud	split
mend	far	grin	stop	early	small	start

1. happy _____

2. fix _____

3. noisy _____

4. raise _____

5. near _____

6. smile _____

7. break _____

8. large _____

9. late _____

10. begin _____

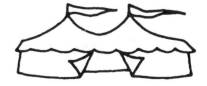

Name _____

Antonyms are words that mean the **opposite**.
   Big and **small** are **antonyms**.
   Hot and **cold** are **antonyms**.

Find a word that means the opposite. Write the number of the antonym on the line provided.

1. right	2. sun	3. laugh	4. dirty
5. day	6. big	7. sad	8. break
9. full		11. float	12. open

_____ moon   _____ fix

_____ happy   _____ sink

_____ empty   _____ left

_____ clean   _____ night

_____ cry   _____ closed

_____ small   _____ under

14

Name _____

Read each sentence. Write an antonym for the word in the box on the line provided.

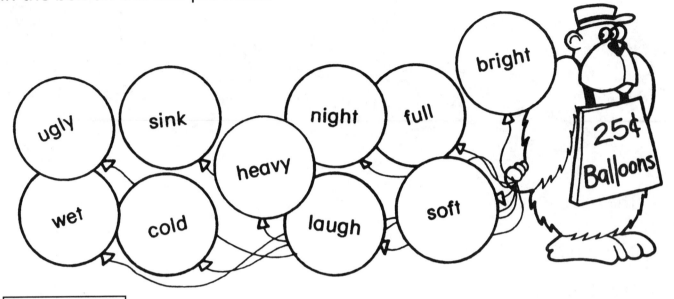

day

1. It is dark at _____

hard

2. The kitten is _____

pretty

3. Monsters are _____

hot

4. Ice cream is _____

float

5. Wood will not _____

light

6. The big rock is _____

dry

7. Snow is cold and _____

cry

8. Clowns make me _____

empty

9. The pool is _____

dark

10. The sun is _____

Name _____

1. The bike is <u>broken</u>.   (fixed)   old   lost

2. Kim is the <u>tallest</u> girl.   oldest   shortest   cutest

3. That <u>boy</u> is nice.   kid   girl   person

4. Steve is very <u>happy</u>.   angry   funny   sad

5. Can Mark <u>work</u> today?   run   play   eat

6. Jump <u>over</u> the net.   under   beside   on

7. I <u>found</u> the door key.   forgot   lost   hid

8. It <u>started</u> on time.   played   showed   stopped

9. I have a <u>hard</u> bed.   big   soft   tiny

10. The movie is <u>short</u>.   long   funny   sad

11. I was <u>early</u> today.   home   lost   late

12. He drives too <u>fast</u>.   slow   hurry   far

Name _____

Use a word from the word box to write an antonym for the underlined word.

1. a <u>sad</u> story   _____

2. a <u>tiny</u> dinosaur   _____

3. an <u>ugly</u> butterfly   _____

4. a <u>sweet</u> lemon   _____

5. a <u>short</u> skyscraper   _____

6. a <u>soft</u> rock   _____

7. a <u>cold</u> dog   _____

8. a <u>thin</u> hippo   _____

9. <u>dirty</u> hands   _____

10. the <u>dim</u> sun   _____

11. a <u>laughing</u> baby   _____

12. a <u>light</u> suitcase   _____

tall	hard
pretty	heavy
hot	huge
bright	fat
happy	clean
crying	sour

Name _____

Read the clues. Write an antonym for each clue word in the puzzle.

Across ➜	**Down** ↓
✓ 1. close	___ 2. yes
___ 3. under	___ 4. left
___ 5. short	___ 6. found
___ 7. bottom	___ 8. push
___ 9. cry	___ 10. love
___ 11. difficult	___ 12. old
___ 13. bad	___ 14. wet

Name _____

Homonyms are words that **sound the same** but **mean different things**.
They are sometimes **spelled differently**, too.

    Know and **no** are **homonyms**.
    Weigh and **way** are **homonyms**.

Write the homonym for each word using a word from the word box.

one	prince	meat	win	berry	mate

meet — _____

_____ — won

bury — _____

_____ — prints

Name _____

Draw a picture of each word in the homonym pairs.

pear — pair

eight — ate

flower — flour

Spectrum Vocabulary Grade 3

Name _____

Write the correct word under each picture.

1. _____
weigh / way

2. _____
son / sun

3. _____
dough / doe

4. _____
flower / flour

5. _____
cheap / cheep

6. _____
stake / steak

7. _____
ate / eight

8. _____
sale / sail

9. _____
male / mail

10. _____
sew / so

11. _____
bare / bear

12. _____
sea / see

13. _____
pare / pear / pair

14. _____
pare / pear / pair

15. _____
pare / pear / pair

Name _____

Write the missing word in each sentence.

flee flea	1. My dog has a _____ on his tail.
	2. Did the cats _____ when the dog barked?

beats beets	3. Mother _____ the eggs with the mixer.
	4. Those _____ are from the garden.

right write	5. Please _____ me a letter soon.
	6. I lost my _____ shoe!

scent cent	7. I like the _____ of the spices.
	8. I have one _____ in my pocket.

won one	9. We _____ the game.
	10. I have _____ dollar in the bank.

dew due	11. The book is _____ on Friday.
	12. The grass is wet from _____ .

no know	13. Do you _____ her name?
	14. There is _____ more candy.

creek creak	15. Frogs live in the _____ .
	16. Does that door _____ when opened?

Spectrum Vocabulary Grade 3

Name _____

Write the missing word on the line provided.

1. My _____ Ted is six.

2. I _____ a hot dog.

3. _____ lost my key.

4. Comb your _____ .

5. I hurt my _____ arm.

6. Pick a _____ .

7. I went last _____ .

8. I _____ a baby bird.

9. My dog eats _____ .

10. Let's _____ the boat.

sun	son
ate	eight
eye	I
hair	hare
right	write
flour	flower
night	knight
see	sea
meat	meet
sale	sail

Name _____

Match the words that sound the same. Write the number beside the word it matches.

1. right	2. bear	3. dear	4. eight
5. cent	6. sea	7. I	8. flour
9. pear	10. so	11. blew	12. ring

_____ eye	_____ write	_____ sew	_____ pair
_____ wring	_____ deer	_____ bare	_____ flower
_____ blue	_____ see	_____ ate	_____ scent

Name _____

Context Clues are clues you can find in a sentence to help you figure out **what a word means**. Read the sentence:

The mouse felt **puny** standing next to the elephant.

Elephants are **big** and **mice** are **small**. That is a **clue** that can help you figure out that **puny** means **little**.

Choose a word from the word box to replace the **boldfaced** word in each sentence. Write it on the line provided.

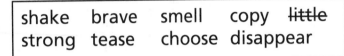

| shake | brave | smell | copy | ~~little~~ |
| strong | tease | choose | disappear | |

1. The mouse felt **puny** standing next to the elephant.

   little
   _____

2. Sour milk can have a bad **odor**.

   _____

3. I get mad when big kids **taunt** my sister.

   _____

4. The people will **elect** a new president.

   _____

5. It was so cold I began to **quiver**.

   _____

6. These trees look **sturdy** enough to climb.

   _____

7. I saw the light in the distance **vanish**.

   _____

8. My brother can **imitate** the sound of a bird.

   _____

9. The **courageous** knight fought the mean dragon.

   _____

Choose a word from the word box to replace the **boldfaced** word in each sentence.

trade	smile	hit	shine	path
spin	move	burn	extra	dressed

1. She can really **whack** the ball. _____

2. The dancer began to **twirl**. _____

3. I couldn't **budge** the heavy box. _____

4. The teacher said to **exchange** papers. _____

5. The silly joke made him **grin**. _____

6. A hot iron can **scorch** clothes. _____

7. The **spare** tire is in the trunk. _____

8. We followed the **trail** back to camp. _____

9. Waxing the car made is **gleam**. _____

10. The king was **clad** in royal robes. _____

Name _____

Read this story about learning to skate. Then answer the questions.

Many times I had **longed** to be able to ice skate. Finally my big sister agreed to teach me.

I was filled with **glee** as I laced up my skates for the first time. I thought I would be **gliding** over the ice in minutes. Was I surprised when I stood up and fell right on the ice. It sure was **chilly**!

My sister helped me up and said, "Don't **fret**. After a few more **tumbles** you'll be skating like a star!"

1. Which **boldfaced** word in the story means:

a. cold? _____

b. wished? _____

c. joy? _____

d. worry? _____

e. moving? _____

f. falls? _____

2. Circle the best answer.

a. The word **chilly** has to do with

food   temperature   skates

b. Which would most likely fill you with **glee**?

being sick   a surprise party

c. Which would you most likely **long** for?

a missing toy   a broken pencil

d. When would you be most likely to **fret**?

if you missed the school bus   if you got a good grade

Name _____

Read each pair of words below. Choose the correct word for each sentence. Write the word on the line provided.

metal—shiny, hard material
through—in one side and out the other
then—at that time

medal—an award
thorough—complete
than—a comparison

---

1. Mom told me to do a

   _____

   job of cleaning
   my room.

   through   thorough

4. The railroad track went

   _____

   a long tunnel.

   through   thorough

---

2. The dog barked,

   _____

   he wagged his tail.

   then   than

5. My new bike is bigger

   _____

   my old one.

   then   than

---

3. I got a

   _____

   for the first place in
   the contest.

   medal   metal

6. The tent was made of cloth with

   _____

   poles.

   medal   metal

Name _____

Read each pair of words below. Choose the correct word for each sentence.
Write the word on the line provided.

quite—very   **quiet**—not noisy
loose—not tight   **lose**—misplace
guest—visitor   **guessed**—made a guess

1. We had a _____ for dinner.
   guest   guessed

2. I promise not to _____ the note.
   loose   lose

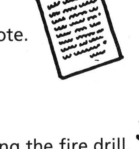

3. The children kept _____ during the fire drill.
   quite   quiet

4. The weather was _____ hot yesterday.
   quite   quiet

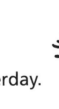

5. The children _____ who was behind the mask.
   guest   guessed

6. My tooth was _____ so I didn't want to eat
   an apple.   lose   loose

Name _____

Concept words are words that have to do with a certain **topic** or **idea**.

    One, subtract, and **ten** are all **math** words.

    Umpire, shortstop, base, and **home run** are all **baseball** words.

Read the words in the word box. Then find the correct word for each sentence. Write the word in the boxes.

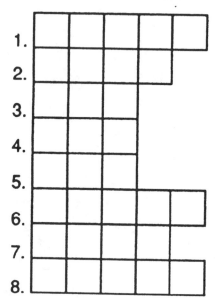

Three
one
Four
eight
two
Seven
six
five

1. Do you know the story of "The _____ Little Pigs"?

2. _____ and four are eight.

3. Which one of the _____ puzzles do you want—the large one or the small one?

4. Three and three are _____.

5. Today is the baby's first birthday; she is _____ year old.

6. Do you like to play _____ Up?

7. Mom says to be home for dinner by _____ o'clock.

8. I go to bed at _____ o'clock.

Name _____

Read this story full of **social studies words**.
Write each **boldfaced** word next to its
meaning.

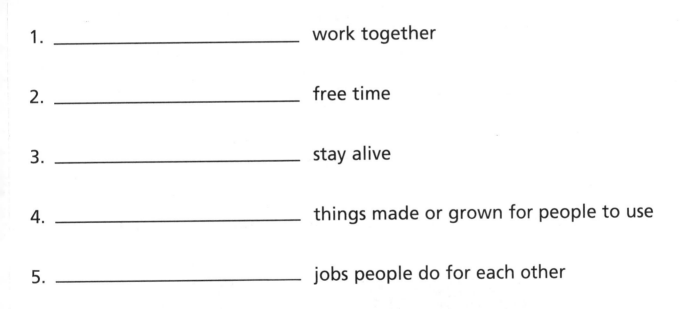

People everywhere have the same
needs. They all need food, clothing, and
shelter to **survive**, or stay alive.

In a community people **cooperate**, or
work together, to get the things they need.

Some people provide **goods**, which are things made or grown for people
to use. Other people provide **services**, or jobs that help others.

Besides needs, there are many things people want to make their lives
more comfortable or fun. They buy many goods and services to enjoy in their
leisure, or free time.

1. _____ work together

2. _____ free time

3. _____ stay alive

4. _____ things made or grown for people to use

5. _____ jobs people do for each other

These pictures show jobs people do. Label them **goods** or **services**.

6.

7.

_____   _____

Read this story full of **science words**. Write each **boldfaced** word next to its meaning.

    Scientists are looking for new **sources**, or places, to get energy. They are finding new ways to make, or **produce**, the power we will need in the future.

    One kind of energy is **geothermal**. "Geo" means "earth" and "thermal" means "heat." Geothermal energy comes from heat that is already stored inside the earth.

    Another kind of energy is **solar**. "Sol" means "sun." The sunlight is changed into energy we can use.

1. _____ heat from the earth

2. _____ from the sun

3. _____ to make

4. _____ places to get something

These pictures show kinds of energy. Label them **geothermal** or **solar**.

5. _____   6. _____

Name _____

Read the list of **science words** in the word box. Write each word in the correct list.

BETTER GRADES THRU SCIENCE!

fishing pole	hummingbird
stinkbug	poodle
telephone	aquarium
television	redwood tree
mushroom	roller skates
laser beam	space shuttle
meteor	tadpole
toucan	crocodile
warthog	walkie-talkie

Living

_____

_____

_____

_____

_____

_____

_____

Non-Living

_____

_____

_____

_____

_____

_____

_____

Name _____

Read this passage full of **computer words**.

    Computers may seem "smart" but they cannot think. The only thing they can do is follow a set of instructions called a **program** which must be written by a person. The computer **hardware** (machinery) and **software** (programs) work together.

    For the computer to work, a person must enter **data**, or information, into the computer. This is called **input**. New data is entered by typing on a **keyboard** that has letters and symbols like a typewriter. Data may be stored on a **disk** which is used to record and save information.

    Next, the computer "reads" the data and follows the instructions of the program. The program may tell it to organize the data, compare it to other data, or store it for later use. This is called data **processing**.

    When the processing is complete, the computer can display the results either on the screen or printed on paper as a **printout**.

Find and write a **boldfaced** word from the story for each description.

1. _____ used to save and record information

2. _____ organizing, comparing, or storing data

3. _____ results printed on paper

4. _____ set of instructions for a computer

5. _____ computer machinery

6. _____ entering data

7. _____ computer programs

8. _____ where data is entered

Spectrum Vocabulary Grade 3

Name _____

Sensory words are words that describe something you **smell, taste, touch, see** or **hear**.

Match the sense with the sensory word.

see	noisy
touch	soft
hear	stinky
smell	bright
taste	sweet

Write a sentence using each of the sensory words above.

1. _____

2. _____

3. _____

4. _____

5. _____

Name _____

Rewrite each sentence using two sensory words from the word box.

beautiful	sweet	boring
shiny	kind	tired
red	huge	stinky
fluffy	tiny	spotted
old	colorful	new
young	brown	broken
puppy	thrilling	exciting

1. I saw a butterfly.

_____

2. I have a dog.

_____

3. We saw a movie.

_____

4. This is my bike.

_____

5. My friend is.

_____

Name _____

Fill in each line with sensory words to complete the poem.

I see _____

_____

I hear _____

_____

I taste _____

_____

I smell _____

_____

I feel _____

_____

Name _____

Onomatopoeia is a word that **describes a sound**.
Clack, boom, and **splash** are all **onomatopoeia**.

Choose a word from the word box that describes the picture.

sizzle	pop	moo	whir
hiss	whine	oink	howl

1. _____

2. _____

3. _____

4. _____

5. _____

6. _____

7. _____

8. _____

Name _____

Read each onomatopoeia word in the word box. Write a sentence for each word describing how the noise was made.

clop	splash
pop	bang
squeak	buzz

1. _____

_____

2. _____

_____

3. _____

_____

4. _____

_____

5. _____

_____

6. _____

_____

Name _____

A **plural** word is **more than one** of a person, place, or thing.

The **plural** form of **nurse** is **nurses**.

The **plural** form of **city** is **cities**.

The **plural** form of **bag** is **bags**.

Add an **s** to the end of each word to make it plural.

1. rabbit _____

2. duck _____

3. horse _____

4. cow _____

5. rooster _____

6. pig _____

7. llama _____

8. chick _____

9. goat _____

10. hamster_____

Name _____

Change each word to the plural form. Write the word on the line.
Change **f** to **v** and add **es**.
Change **y** to **i** and add **es**.

1. The _____ are pretty colors.
   leaf

2. We picked _____ in the woods.
   berry

3. We saw a movie about _____ .
   wolf

4. The _____ are in the barn.
   calf

5. There are two _____ in the city.
   library

6. Dad built _____ in the garage.
   shelf

7. It costs a dollar to ride the _____ .
   pony

8. The story is about seven tiny _____ .
   elf

9. _____ are fun to watch at night.
   Firefly

10. Mother planted _____ in the yard.
    lily

11. The mother lion has three _____ .
    baby

12. The police caught the _____ .
    thief

Name _____

Write each word in the plural form.
When a word ends in **ch**, **sh**, or **x**, add **es**.
Remember to change **y** to **i** and add **es**.

1. bunny   _____

2. story   _____

3. penny   _____

4. city   _____

5. brush   _____

6. size   _____

7. match   _____

8. mailbox   _____

Name _____

Write the plural form of each word next to its picture.
When a word ends in **vowel-o,** add **s.**
When a word ends in **consonant-o,** add **es.**

1. _____

2. _____

3. _____

4. _____

5. _____

6. _____

Name _____

Some words have **irregular plurals**. Read the words in the word box. Write the plural form of the <u>underlined</u> word on the line to complete each sentence.

geese	women	cattle	oxen
men	moose	mice	children

1. The <u>child</u> _____ rode the bus to school.

2. All those <u>man</u> _____ are running in the race tomorrow.

3. Have you seen the <u>goose</u> _____ flying over head?

4. The team of <u>ox</u> _____ pulled the plow.

5. These <u>woman</u> _____ are all famous.

6. The <u>mouse</u> _____ in the garage have built a nest.

7. We saw <u>moose</u> _____ at the zoo.

8. Those <u>cattle</u> _____ roam for miles on the ranch.

Name _____

A **suffix** is a part **added to the end** of a word. Suffixes change the meanings of words.

In the word **packing**, **ing** is the **suffix**.
In the word **wonderful**, **ful** is the **suffix**.

Add the suffix **ing** to a word from the word box to complete each sentence. Write the word on the line provided.

1. He is _____ questions.

2. We have been _____ clothes.

3. John has been _____ Father with the car.

4. Is Mother _____ dinner?

5. Mark is _____ weeds from the garden.

6. Is Nancy _____ all the doors?

7. Are you _____ to the store?

8. Get your pole and let's go _____ .

9. The children were _____ too loudly.

10. I have been _____ in bed all day.

Name _____

Add the suffix **ed** to a word from the word box to complete each sentence.
Write the word on the line provided.

1. Mother _____ the baby to sleep.

2. We _____ all the carrot seeds.

3. Bill and John _____ open all the nuts.

4. That mule _____ me!

5. Susan _____ up the tree.

6. Our dog _____ all night long.

7. Father _____ our new car on the street.

8. Mary _____ the wall all blue.

9. It _____ cats and dogs today.

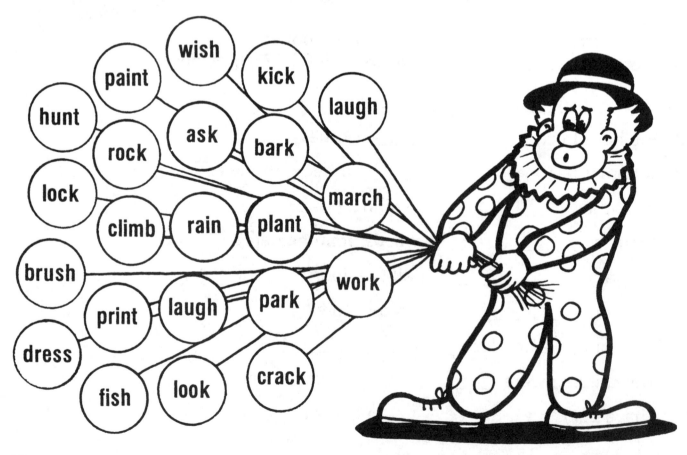

Spectrum Vocabulary Grade 3

Name _____

Add the suffix **ful** to a word from the word box to complete each sentence. Write the word on the line provided.

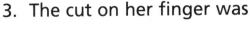

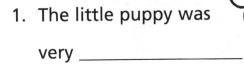
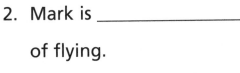

Where do you want it?

play cheer help
care mind joy
harm pain rest
color use cup
fear thank hope

1. The little puppy was

   very _____ .

2. Mark is _____

   of flying.

3. The cut on her finger was

   _____ .

4. Be _____
   with that hot iron.

5. We are _____ we will get a new car.

6. Nancy is always so nice and _____ .

7. The peacock is a _____ bird.

8. Ann is very _____ to her mother.

9. A snake could be _____ .

10. Mother had a very _____ nap.

11. They are _____ the fire was not bad.

Name _____

Circle the suffix **less** or **ness** to complete each sentence.

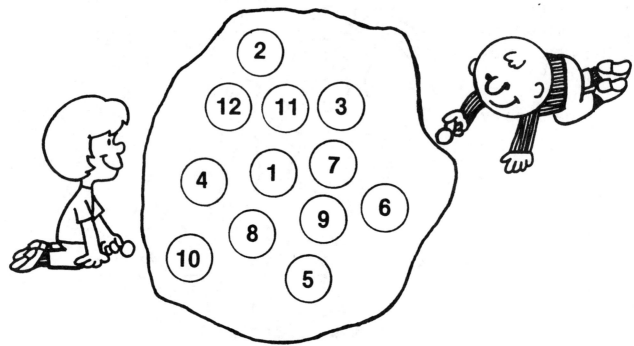

1. The dark_____ scared us.   less   ness

2. I never had good grades in neat_____.   less   ness

3. The shot was pain_____.   less   ness

4. Oh, for good_____ sakes!   less   ness

5. The poor dog was home_____.   less   ness

6. The soft_____ of cotton feels good.   less   ness

7. This old toy is use_____.   less   ness

8. She loves the sweet_____ of oranges.   less   ness

9. Our new car is spot_____.   less   ness

10. His coat's thick_____ kept him warm.   less   ness

11. Don't be so care_____!   less   ness

12. Now I am tooth_____!   less   ness

Name _____

Add the suffix **ly** to the best word for each sentence. Write the word on the line provided.

1. Please don't talk so _____ !

2. We must walk _____ or we'll be late.

3. That car _____ ran into us!

4. Daniel is a very _____ boy.

5. This traffic is moving too _____ !

6. I can't see the boat _____ in this fog.

7. The baby is asleep. Play _____ .

8. "What a _____ present," said Mother.

9. "You have _____ touched your dinner," said Dad.

10. The fireman _____ saved the little girl.

11. I will _____ do that for you.

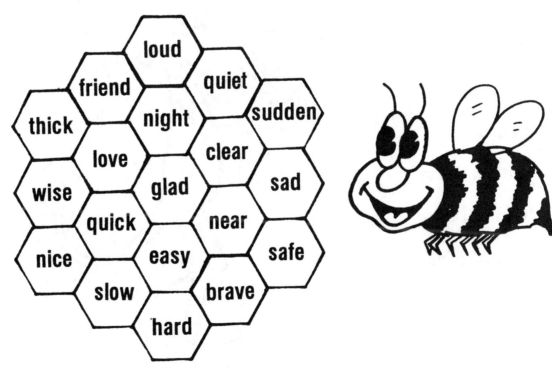

Name _____

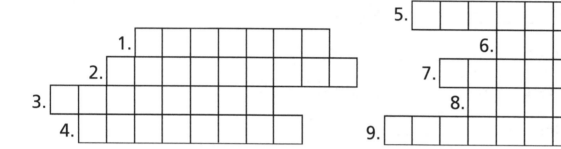

sadly   friendless   sweetly

lifeless   cheerful   needless

nearly   toothless   careful

Find the word in the word box that matches each meaning below. Fill in the puzzle.

1. with sweetness

2. no teeth

3. full of cheer

4. do not need

5. doing with care

6. almost

7. with sadness

8. without life

9. without friends

Name _____

A **prefix** is a part **added to the beginning** of a word. Prefixes change the meanings of words.

The **prefix** in **beside** is **be**.
The **prefix** in **impossible** is **im**.

Color the picture using the prefix code.

Prefix Code	
be — yellow	**a** — red
mis — blue	**sub** — orange

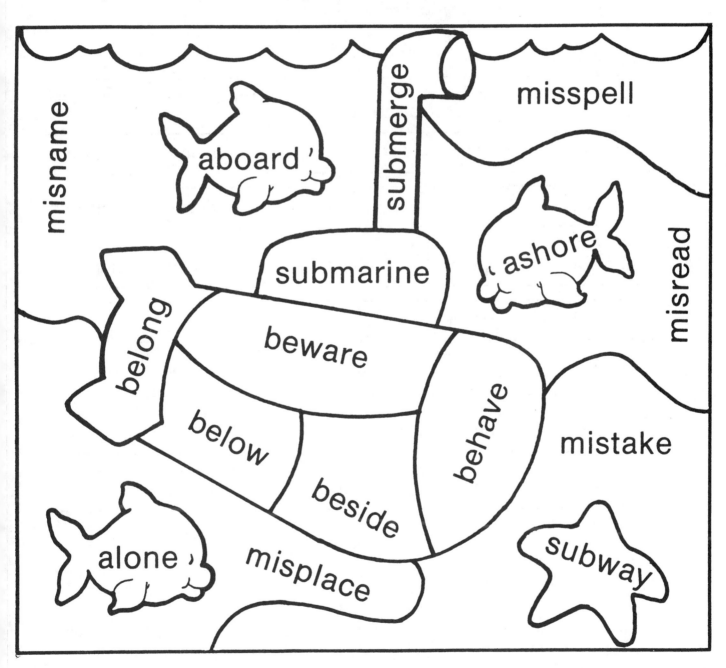

Name _____

Circle the words in each row that have the same prefix.

1. | unclear | unhappy | enjoy | uncommon | uncertain |

2. | export | enter | exit | exhale | exclaim |

3. | disappear | dislike | disobey | deliver | discount |

4. | nonstop | nonsense | never | nonsmoking | nonpaying |

5. | precook | preview | perfect | prevent | prepay |

6. | redo | repaint | redraw | raise | replay |

7. | midnight | muddy | midday | midpoint | midland |

8. | inhale | into | incorrect | important | inside |

Name _____

Read the prefix at the beginning of each row. Circle the prefix in each word in the row.

1.	un	unsafe	unkind	unbend	undone

2.	dis	dislike	discolor	disown	disobey

3.	in	indoor	input	inborn	into

4.	re	relive	redo	regain	repay

5.	mis	mistake	misprint	misspell	misname

6.	im	impolite	imperfect	improper	impossible

7.	non	nonsense	nonstop	nonfat	nonliving

8.	ex	explain	exhale	exclaim	export

Name _____

Read each word. Write the prefix in the **Prefix** column and the word without the prefix in the **Word** column.

	Prefix	Word
1. bicycle		
2. delay		
3. forearm		
4. export		
5. adjust		
6. research		
7. unclean		
8. misprint		
9. relive		
10. telephone		
11. uneven		
12. repaint		

Name _____

Read each word. Write the prefix in the **Prefix** column and the word without the prefix in the **Word** column.

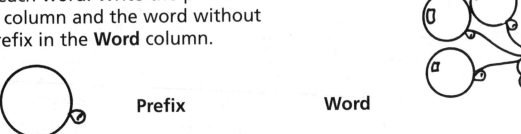

	Prefix	Word
1. aboard	_____	_____
2. replay	_____	_____
3. unkind	_____	_____
4. inside	_____	_____
5. below	_____	_____
6. preschool	_____	_____
7. mistake	_____	_____
8. nonsense	_____	_____
9. impress	_____	_____
10. dismiss	_____	_____

Name _____

Write each word under the correct heading. Circle the prefix or suffix in each word.

windy	floating	subway	rewrite
fearless	unclear	hilly	except
inside	nonsense	kindness	painted
beaches	hopeful	rename	precook

Words With Prefixes

_____   _____

_____   _____

_____   _____

_____   _____

Words With Suffixes

_____   _____

_____   _____

_____   _____

Spectrum Vocabulary Grade 3

Name _____

A **root** or **base word** is the word that is left after you **take off a prefix or suffix**.
A base word **can stand on its own**.
Side is the base word of **inside**.
Nerve is the base word of **nervous**.

A root word **cannot stand on its own**.
Cept is the root word of **except**.
Cess is the root word of **recess**.

Replace the <u>underlined</u> base word by adding a suffix to complete each sentence.

1. We go ice <u>skate</u> during the winter.   _____

2. Mom <u>bake</u> a cake for all of us.   _____

3. Who <u>clean</u> off the table?   _____

4. Are you <u>have</u> a good time?   _____

5. Our dog has four <u>leg</u>.   _____

6. Mike went to two <u>party</u> this week.   _____

Circle the base word in each group.

1. preview   viewing   view

2. redo   did   do

3. liked   like   dislike

4. disagree   agreed   agree

5. called   call   calling

6. unrest   resting   rest

Name _____

Some prefixes are added to root or base words to tell how many. Use the prefixes in the word box to complete each sentence. Then write the definition in the blank beside each prefix.

uni-_____	tri-_____	deca-_____
bi-_____	quadr-_____	

1. **Cycle** is a Greek word for circle or wheel. A two-wheeled vehicle is called a _____. Therefore, the **prefix bi-** means _____.

   Young children ride a three-wheeled vehicle called a _____.

   The **prefix tri-** means _____.

   A vehicle that has just one wheel is called a _____.

   Therefore, the **prefix uni-** means _____.

2. **Ped** or **pod** are root words meaning foot. A **biped** is an animal with _____ feet.

   The horse is a **quadruped**. It has _____ feet.

   Our camera stand is called a **tripod**. It has _____ feet.

3. A shape with ten sides is called a **decagon**. Therefore the **prefix deca-** means _____.

   A **decapod** is an animal with _____ legs and feet.

4. A **tricolor** is a flag with _____ colors.

5. A **unicorn** has _____ horn.

6. A school **uniform** is made in _____ style for all students.

7. A **trimester** contains _____ months.

8. A **quadruplet** is one of _____ children born at the same time.

9. A **bilingual** person speaks _____ languages.

10. A **triangle** has _____ sides and _____ angles.

Name _____

	port	to bring, to carry

deport	to expel or send away from a country (from Latin *de-*, "away")
export	to send goods to another country (from Latin *ex-*, "out, out of")
import	to bring in from an outside source, especially from a foreign country (from Latin *in-*, "in")
portfolio	a flat case for carrying papers, manuscripts, drawings, or other documents (from Latin *folium*, "a leaf")

Fill in each blank with a word from the word box.

1. The artist kept her sketches in a leather _____.

2. People without official immigration papers can be _____(ed) to their home countries.

3. The United States _____(s) oil from the Middle East.

Circle the root that means **to bring, to carry** in each word. Then write a brief definition on the line provided.

1. transportation _____

2. reporter _____

3. porter _____

4. supportive _____

5. portable _____

Name _____

scope	**to look**

kaleidoscope	a tube-shaped toy that one looks through to see a variety of changing colored patterns
microscope	an instrument for viewing objects too small to be seen by the naked eye
periscope	an instrument for viewing objects that are out of sight — used especially in submarines
scope	range of view or understanding; the space within which something exists, covers, or is limited to

Match each word with its use.

_____ kaleidoscope   1. objects that are out of sight

_____ microscope   2. colored patterns

_____ periscope   3. extremely small objects

Write the word from the word box that best completes each sentence on the line provided.

1. The biologist used a _____ to help with her research.
2. Jerry enjoyed the colors and patterns in his _____.
3. Once the submarine was under water, the crew relied on the _____ to see what was on the surface.
4. A detailed history of the periscope is out of the _____ of the dictionary.

List four things that you would need to see with a microscope.

_____   _____

_____   _____

Name _____

phon, phone	sound

megaphone	a funnel-shaped device for making sounds louder
microphone	an instrument that changes sound waves into electrical signals for transmission or amplification
phonetic	having to do with speech sounds
phonics	the rules of sound used in teaching reading and word pronunciation
xylophone	a percussion instrument made of tuned wooden bars struck with small hand-held hammers

Circle the root word that means **sound** in the following words.

1. microphone
2. xylophone
3. phonics
4. megaphone
5. phonetic

Write the word from the word box that best completes each sentence on the line provided.

1. Tyler learned to play the _____ in music class.

2. Even with the _____ , it was hard to hear the cheerleaders over the crowd.

3. The singer used a headset _____ so her hands would be free for dancing.

4. We learned about the sounds of "c" in _____ class.

Name _____

-logy	**the study of**

archeology	the study of the life and culture of ancient people
meteorology	the study of weather
psychology	the study of the human mind and behavior
seismology	the study of earthquakes
zoology	the study of animals

Circle the root that means **the study of** in the following words.

1. zoology
2. psychology
3. archeology
4. meteorology
5. seismology

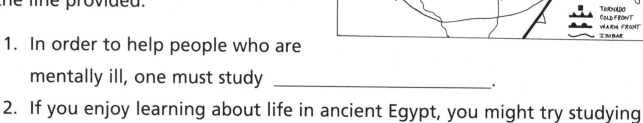

Write the word from the word box that best completes each sentence on the line provided.

1. In order to help people who are

   mentally ill, one must study _____.

2. If you enjoy learning about life in ancient Egypt, you might try studying

   _____.

3. To plan activities for a vacation, it would be helpful to know something

   about _____ in order to bring the right clothes.

4. If you are interested in animals, you could take up the study of

   _____.

5. If you lived in California, it might be wise to know something about

   _____ so that you would understand what was

   happening when the earth trembled.

Name _____

Imported words are words used in English that come from **different languages,** such as Greek, Latin, French, or German.

Parka is a **Siberian** word.

Pamper is a **Dutch** word.

Write each word from the word box next to its definition.

vanilla (Spanish)	khaki (Hindi)
shampoo (Hindi)	crayon (French)
question (French)	cafeteria (Spanish)

1. A _____ means to ask or seek.

2. _____ is a soap used on hair.

3. A _____ is a piece of colored wax.

4. _____ describes a color or a type of fabric.

5. A _____ is a place to eat lunch.

6. _____ is a flavoring used in desserts like ice cream and cookies.

Now write sentences using two of the words from above.

1. _____

_____

2. _____

_____

Name _____

Use the French words from the word box to complete the sentences.

chef: someone who cooks
buffet: many different foods on one table
beret: a small hat
catalogue: magazine of things for sale
budget: a list setting aside money for bills, food, and other things
ballet: a type of dance

1. My older sister wears a _____ when it is

   cold out.

2. I got this new _____ of video games in the mail.

 3. Some of the football players are taking _____

   to become more graceful.

4. There are fried rice, sweet and sour chicken, and egg rolls on

   the _____.

5. The _____ at this restaurant used to work

   with a very famous cook.

6. How much money did we _____ for the birthday gift?

Name _____

Read each sentence. Match the Arabic and Spanish words to their definitions.

At sunset the sky was pink, **crimson**, and orange.

The **asphalt** in the parking lot was very hot.

Dad got a blue **brocade** sofa for the living room.

The workers filled the truck with its **cargo** of fresh vegetables.

The **bronco** tried to throw off its rider.

Mom got a new **amber** ring for her birthday.

_____ 1. a stone made of fossilized tree sap

_____ 2. a rich fabric used in curtains or furniture

_____ 3. a deep red color

_____ 4. a type of horse

_____ 5. suitcases, boxes, or other things a plane or truck may carry

_____ 6. another word for black top or pavement

a.   amber (Arabic)

b.   crimson (Arabic)

c.   asphalt (Arabic)

d.   cargo (Spanish)

e.   bronco (Spanish)

f.   brocade (Spanish)

Name _____

Read the definitions of each word. Write a sentence using each word on the lines provided.

1. chocolate (Aztec)   a substance made from the cocoa plant used to make candy

_____

2. clan (Italian)   family group

_____

3. mango (Malaysian) a sweet, tropical, oval-shaped fruit

_____

4. tycoon (Chinese)   a very rich person

_____

5. waffle (Dutch)   a hot breakfast food made in an iron that shapes the batter

_____

6. jazz (African)   an American type of music

_____

Complete each phrase with an imported food word from the word box.

bread (Old English)	shrimp (German)
pizza (Latin)	mushroom (French)
broccoli (Italian)	omelet (French)
ketchup (Chinese)	vegetable (Latin)

1. Wheat, white, rye, cinnamon-raisin _____

2. Grows in the woods and tastes great on pizza _____

3. Beans, cauliflower, lettuce, peppers are all

   types of _____.

4. Made of eggs and filled with cheese and vegetables _____

5. Comes from the Latin word for "pound" because that's what you do with

   the dough _____

6. A tomato-flavored sauce to put on your burgers and fries

   _____

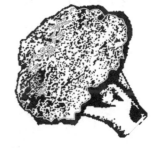

7. A green vegetable that looks like cauliflower

   _____

8. Take off the tails of these shellfish before you eat _____.

Name _____

An **abbreviation** is the **shortened** version of a word.

Read the words and their abbreviations in the word box.

Sunday—Sun.	January—Jan.
Monday—Mon.	February—Feb.
Tuesday—Tues.	March—Mar.
Wednesday—Wed.	April—Apr.
Thursday—Thurs.	August—Aug.
Friday—Fri.	September—Sept.
Saturday—Sat.	October—Oct.
	November—Nov.
	December—Dec.

Unscramble the abbreviations for the days of the week.

1. tsa _____

2. nus _____

3. onm _____

4. edw _____

5. sute _____

6. rif _____

7. rstuh _____

Unscramble the abbreviations for the months of the year.

1. bef _____

2. mra _____

3. ced _____

4. tco _____

5. rap _____

6. vno _____

Name _____

Write the letter of the abbreviation next to the word it matches.

street—St.	boulevard—Blvd.
yard—yd.	miles per hour—mph
foot—ft.	highway—hwy
mount—Mt.	apartment—apt.
avenue—Ave.	road—Rd.

_____	1.	boulevard	a. mph
_____	2.	street	b. St.
_____	3.	highway	c. yd.
_____	4.	miles per hour	d. Blvd.
_____	5.	road	e. Ave.
_____	6.	avenue	f. ft.
_____	7.	apartment	g. Rd.
_____	8.	mount	h. Mt.
_____	9.	foot	i. hwy
_____	10.	yard	j. apt.

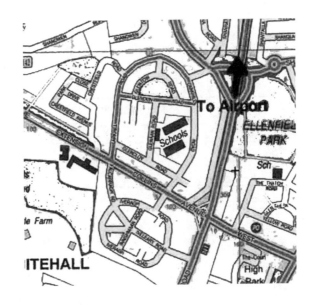

Name _____

Rewrite Emilio's birthday invitation using abbreviations. Rewrite all the numbers as numerals.

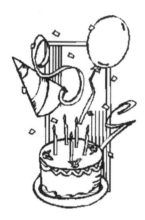

What: Emilio's Tenth Birthday Party

When: Friday, March Seventeenth at Three of the clock

Where: Twenty-seven Oakstream Avenue

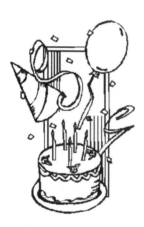

What: _____

When: _____

Where: _____

Name _____

Rewrite each measurement using abbreviations.

1. 7 pounds   _____

2. 5 ounces   _____

3. 3 feet   _____

4. 6 yards   _____

5. 11 inches   _____

6. 2 centimeters   _____

7. 35 miles per hour _____

8. 2 dozen   _____

pounds:	lb.
miles per hour:	mph
ounces:	oz.
yards:	yd.
feet:	ft.
dozen:	doz.
centimeters:	cm
inches:	in.

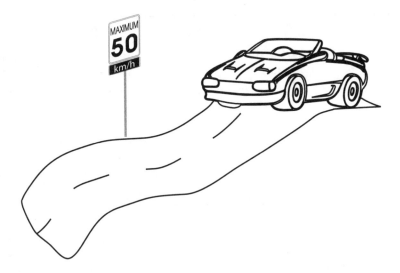

Name _____

Write the day of the week and the date of each calendar event without abbreviations on the lines provided.

Jan.						
Sun.	Mon.	Tue.	Wed.	Thurs.	Fri.	Sat.
13	14 Evan's Birthday!	15 soccer 4 pm	16	17 dentist appt. 5:30 pm	18 Evan's Birthday Party 7 pm	19 Girl Scout mtg. 2 pm

Oct.						
Sun.	Mon.	Tue.	Wed.	Thurs.	Fri.	Sat.
20	21	22 piano lessons	23 soccer 4 pm	24	25	26 piano recital 6 pm
27	28 soccer 4 pm	29	30	31 Mom's Birthday!		

1. _____

2. _____

3. _____

4. _____

5. _____

6. _____

7. _____

8. _____

9. _____

10. _____

Name _____

A **compound word** is **made of two words** than can stand alone.
   Cupcake is a **compound word**.

Match a word from the bottom of the page with a word from the side of the page to make a compound word. Write the words on the lines provided.

1. _____

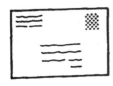

2. _____

3. _____

4. _____

5. _____

Name _____

Make a compound word from two words. Write the compound word.

1. flag + pole

_____

2. base + ball

_____

3. dog + house

_____

4. butter + fly

_____

5. hair + brush

_____

6. lady + bug

_____

7. bare + foot

_____

8. 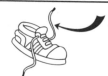 shoe + lace

_____

9. play + pen

_____

10. cup + cake

_____

Name _____

Write the two words that make up each compound word.

1. 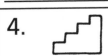 blueberry

_____ _____

2.  popcorn

_____ _____

3. 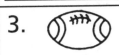 football

_____ _____

4. downstairs

_____ _____

5. sidewalk

_____ _____

6. beehive

_____ _____

7. raincoat

_____ _____

8. snowstorm

_____ _____

9. outside

_____ _____

10. cowboy

_____ _____

Name _____

Make crazy compound words by mixing up the compound words in the word box to make new ones. Write the word on the line and then draw a picture. The first one is done for you.

goldfish	mailbox	cheeseburger
eggshell	broomstick	treetop
hairbrush	junkyard	popcorn
snowman	seaweed	dishpan

goldfish + broomstick

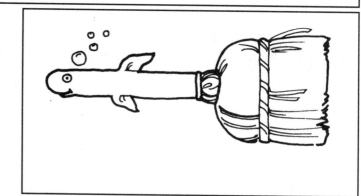

1. ___ **broomfish** ___

2. _____

3. _____

Name _____

Make more crazy compounds! Use the compound words in the box below.

horseshoe	bedroom	rattlesnake
farmhouse	butterfly	moonlight
football	bathtub	scarecrow
arrowhead	starfish	spaceship

1. _____

2. _____

3. _____

Name _____

Complete each sentence using a compound word from the word box.

fireflies	bathtub
scarecrow	cupcakes
campfire	watermelon
crosswalk	volleyball

1. This summer we spent many evenings around the _____.

2. We caught _____ in the dusk.

3. Mom and I baked _____ for the bake sale.

4. Would you like some more _____?

5. Look both ways before using the _____.

6. Can you play _____ after school today?

7. We made a _____ to frighten away the birds that were

    eating the garden.

8. Be careful not to slip when stepping out of the _____.

Name _____

A **contraction** combines two words using an **apostrophe**. Not all of the letters in both words are written.

    We're is the contraction of **we are**; **I'll** is the contraction of **I will**.

Write two words from the word box for each contraction.

should not
will not
has not
I have
we have
you have
is not
do not

isn't

you've

I've

shouldn't

don't

hasn't

won't

we've

Name _____

Write the contraction from the word box in the space provided.

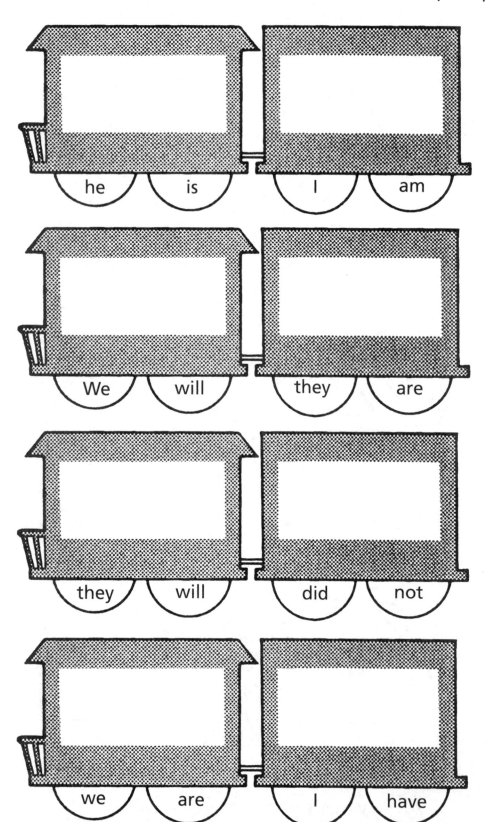

he's
won't
don't
didn't
I'm
we'll
they're
I've
we're
they'll

Spectrum Vocabulary Grade 3

Name _____

Write a contraction of the two words in parentheses.

1. _____ be home soon.
        (I will)

2. Jan _____ play.
        (will not)

3. We _____ ready.
        (are not)

4. That _____ my hat.
        (is not)

5. I think _____ cry.
        (she will)

6. Tod _____ find the cat.
        (did not)

7. _____ like that book.
        (You will)

8. Hurry or _____ be late.
        (we will)

9. Kim _____ live here.
        (does not)

10. _____ ring the bell.
        (They will)

Name _____

Circle the missing words that complete each sentence. Then write the contraction of those words on the line provided.

1. We _____ expecting a big crowd.
   did not   were not

2. Next time _____ come early!
   I will   I am

3. We _____ seen this movie.
   do not   have not

4. I know _____ like it.
   you will   he is

5. This movie _____ for adults.
   can not   is not

6. This line _____ moved.
   has not   we are

7. I _____ want to be last in line!
   is not   would not

8. _____ open soon.
   I am   They will

9. I _____ bring my bubble gum.
   do not   did not

10. _____ worry, we will get seats.
    Could not   Do not

11. Look, _____ selling tickets now.
    we were   they are

12. Ouch, _____ standing on my toe!
    you are   I am

Name _____

Write the contractions.

1. do   not
_____

2. I   will
_____

3. it   is
_____

4. will   not
_____

5. could   not
_____

6. they   are
_____

7. we   are
_____

8. she   is
_____

9. we   will
_____

10. does   not
_____

11. who   is
_____

12. has   not
_____

13. you   are
_____

14. I   am
_____

15. should   not
_____

PAGE 4

Classification is putting objects together in groups.
Lemon, orange, and **lime** are all **fruits.**
Softball, football, and **soccer** are all **sports.**

Cross out the word in each row that does not belong.

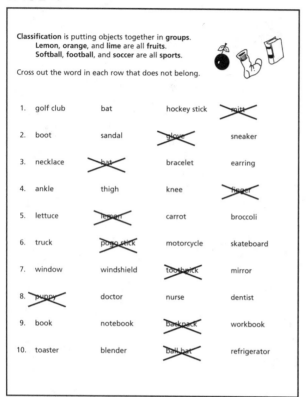

1. golf club   bat   hockey stick   ~~mitt~~
2. boot   sandal   ~~glove~~   sneaker
3. necklace   ~~hat~~   bracelet   earring
4. ankle   thigh   knee   ~~finger~~
5. lettuce   ~~lemon~~   carrot   broccoli
6. truck   ~~pogo stick~~   motorcycle   skateboard
7. window   windshield   ~~toothpick~~   mirror
8. ~~puppy~~   doctor   nurse   dentist
9. book   notebook   ~~backpack~~   workbook
10. toaster   blender   ~~ball bat~~   refrigerator

PAGE 5

Find the title in the word box that best names each group of things listed below. Write the title on the line provided.

| Sounds | Colors | Vegetables | Cities |
| Insects | Shapes | Landforms | Feelings |

1. **Vegetables**
   carrots, broccoli, peas, beans, asparagus

2. **Cities**
   Boston, Dallas, Detroit, Miami, Denver

3. **Sounds**
   pop, bang, whoosh, crash, splat

4. **Shapes**
   circle, rectangle, triangle, square, oval

5. **Colors**
   purple, tan, maroon, turquoise, yellow

6. **Feelings**
   lonely, excited, worried, surprised, scared

7. **Landforms**
   mountains, valleys, hills, plateaus, plains

8. **Insects**

PAGE 6

Cross out the word in each row that does not belong.

1. pine   oak   fir   ~~daisy~~
2. frog   ~~rock~~   flower   tree
3. height   weight   ~~eyes~~   length
4. ~~color~~   ice   steam   water
5. marker   ~~coupon~~   pencil   pen
6. blue   yellow   red   ~~black~~
7. apple   cherry   ~~leaf~~   banana
8. ant   spider   bee   ~~squirrel~~
9. stripe   polka dots   ~~pants~~   plaid
10. viola   ~~drums~~   cello   violin
11. cloud   rain   thunder   ~~wave~~
12. river   stream   creek   ~~ocean~~

PAGE 7

Use the words from the word box to complete each list of animal homes.

hawk	lion	blue jay
whale	bluebird	robin
polar bear	groundhog	horse
dolphin	tuna	shark

Sky
| robin | blue jay |
| bluebird | hawk |

Sea
| shark | tuna |
| dolphin | whale |

Land
| horse | groundhog |
| lion | polar bear |

PAGE 8

Look at each group of words below. First cross out the word that does not belong. Then add a word from the word box that does belong.

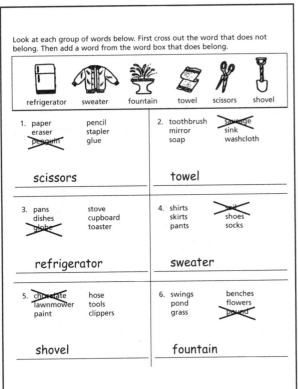

refrigerator sweater fountain towel scissors shovel

1. paper   pencil
   eraser   stapler
   ~~penguin~~ glue

   scissors

2. toothbrush ~~sausage~~
   mirror   sink
   soap   washcloth

   towel

3. pans   stove
   dishes   cupboard
   ~~globe~~ toaster

   refrigerator

4. shirts   ~~oil~~
   skirts   shoes
   pants   socks

   sweater

5. ~~chocolate~~ hose
   lawnmower   tools
   paint   clippers

   shovel

6. swings   benches
   pond   flowers
   grass   ~~pound~~

   fountain

PAGE 9

Synonyms are words that mean the **same** thing. **Big** and **huge** are **synonyms**. **Tiny** and **small** are **synonyms**.

Circle the two words in each row that mean the same thing.

1. (easy)   (simple)   funny
2. (tiny)   baby   (small)
3. dance   (jump)   (leap)
4. (bumpy) (rough)   heavy
5. hear   (look)   (watch)
6. (fix)   (repair)   buy
7. stop   (start)   (begin)
8. (quick) (fast)   run
9. (smile) happy   (grin)
10. (close) (shut)   open
11. fence   (home)   (house)
12. (mean) (nasty)   big

PAGE 10

Read each sentence. Write a word from the word box that has almost the same meaning as the underlined word.

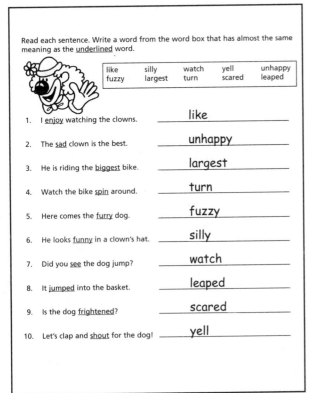

| like | silly | watch | yell | unhappy |
| fuzzy | largest | turn | scared | leaped |

1. I _enjoy_ watching the clowns.   **like**
2. The _sad_ clown is the best.   **unhappy**
3. He is riding the _biggest_ bike.   **largest**
4. Watch the bike _spin_ around.   **turn**
5. Here comes the _furry_ dog.   **fuzzy**
6. He looks _funny_ in a clown's hat.   **silly**
7. Did you _see_ the dog jump?   **watch**
8. It _jumped_ into the basket.   **leaped**
9. Is the dog _frightened_?   **scared**
10. Let's clap and _shout_ for the dog!   **yell**

PAGE 11

Choose a word from the word box that could take the place of the **bold-faced** word in each sentence. Write it on the line provided.

| thick | whole | help | choose | careful | piece |

1. I will **select** a new tie for Dad.

   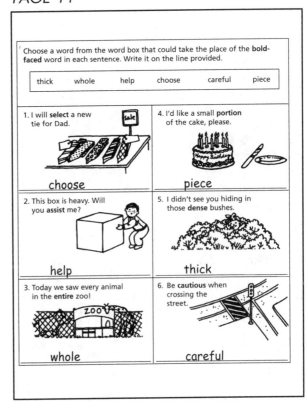

   choose

2. This box is heavy. Will you **assist** me?

   help

3. Today we saw every animal in the **entire** zoo!

   whole

4. I'd like a small **portion** of the cake, please.

   piece

5. I didn't see you hiding in those **dense** bushes.

   thick

6. Be **cautious** when crossing the street.

   careful

PAGE 12

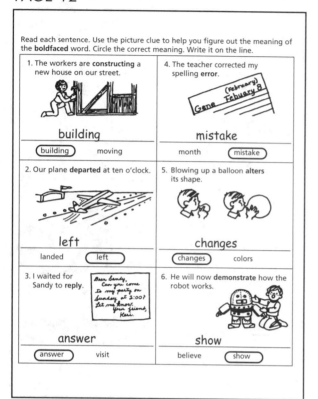

Read each sentence. Use the picture clue to help you figure out the meaning of the **boldfaced** word. Circle the correct meaning. Write it on the line.

1. The workers are **constructing** a new house on our street.

building

(building)   moving

2. Our plane **departed** at ten o'clock.

left

landed   (left)

3. I waited for Sandy to **reply**.

answer

(answer)   visit

4. The teacher corrected my spelling **error**.

mistake

month   (mistake)

5. Blowing up a balloon **alters** its shape.

changes

(changes)   colors

6. He will now **demonstrate** how the robot works.

show

believe   (show)

PAGE 13

Write a synonym for each word using the words from the word box.

tardy	sad	jolly	big	frown	lower	yellow
fat	thin	quiet	lift	close	loud	split
mend	far	grin	stop	early	small	start

1. happy   jolly
2. fix   mend
3. noisy   loud
4. raise   lift
5. near   close
6. smile   grin
7. break   split
8. large   big
9. late   tardy
10. begin   start

PAGE 14

Antonyms are words that mean the **opposite**.
   Big and **small** are **antonyms**.
   Hot and **cold** are **antonyms**.

Find a word that means the opposite. Write the number of the antonym on the line provided.

1. right	2. sun	3. laugh	4. dirty
5. day	6. big	7. sad	8. break
9. full		11. float	12. open

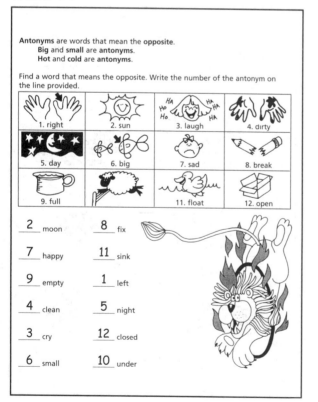

_2_ moon   _8_ fix

_7_ happy   _11_ sink

_9_ empty   _1_ left

_4_ clean   _5_ night

_3_ cry   _12_ closed

_6_ small   _10_ under

PAGE 15

Read each sentence. Write an antonym for the word in the box on the line provided.

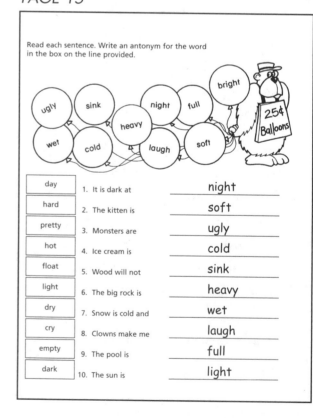

day	1. It is dark at	night
hard	2. The kitten is	soft
pretty	3. Monsters are	ugly
hot	4. Ice cream is	cold
float	5. Wood will not	sink
light	6. The big rock is	heavy
dry	7. Snow is cold and	wet
cry	8. Clowns make me	laugh
empty	9. The pool is	full
dark	10. The sun is	light

PAGE 16

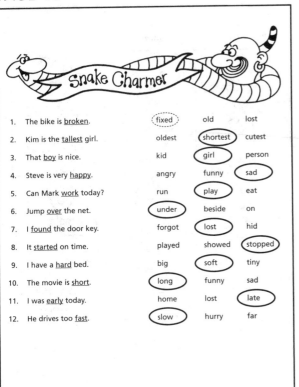

Snake Charmer

1. The bike is <u>broken</u>. — (fixed)   old   lost
2. Kim is the <u>tallest</u> girl. — oldest   (shortest)   cutest
3. That <u>boy</u> is nice. — kid   (girl)   person
4. Steve is very <u>happy</u>. — angry   funny   (sad)
5. Can Mark <u>work</u> today? — run   (play)   eat
6. Jump <u>over</u> the net. — (under)   beside   on
7. I <u>found</u> the door key. — forgot   (lost)   hid
8. It <u>started</u> on time. — played   showed   (stopped)
9. I have a <u>hard</u> bed. — big   (soft)   tiny
10. The movie is <u>short</u>. — (long)   funny   sad
11. I was <u>early</u> today. — home   lost   (late)
12. He drives too <u>fast</u>. — (slow)   hurry   far

PAGE 17

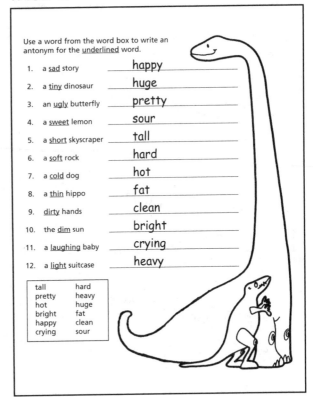

Use a word from the word box to write an antonym for the <u>underlined</u> word.

1. a <u>sad</u> story — happy
2. a <u>tiny</u> dinosaur — huge
3. an <u>ugly</u> butterfly — pretty
4. a <u>sweet</u> lemon — sour
5. a <u>short</u> skyscraper — tall
6. a <u>soft</u> rock — hard
7. a <u>cold</u> dog — hot
8. a <u>thin</u> hippo — fat
9. <u>dirty</u> hands — clean
10. the <u>dim</u> sun — bright
11. a <u>laughing</u> baby — crying
12. a <u>light</u> suitcase — heavy

tall	hard
pretty	heavy
hot	huge
bright	fat
happy	clean
crying	sour

PAGE 18

Read the clues. Write an antonym for each clue word in the puzzle.

Across →	**Down** ↓
✓ 1. close	___ 2. yes
___ 3. under	___ 4. left
___ 5. short	___ 6. found
___ 7. bottom	___ 8. push
___ 9. cry	___ 10. love
___ 11. difficult	___ 12. old
___ 13. bad	___ 14. wet

Crossword answers: Open, over, laugh, easy, tall, top, good

PAGE 19

Homonyms are words that **sound the same** but **mean different things**. They are sometimes **spelled differently**, too.
   Know and **no** are **homonyms**.
   Weigh and **way** are **homonyms**.

Write the homonym for each word using a word from the word box.

one	prince	meat	win	berry	mate

meet — meat   one — won

bury — berry   prince — prints

PAGE 20

Draw a picture of each word in the homonym pairs.

> Pictures will vary.

pear — pair

> Pictures will vary.

eight — ate

> Pictures will vary.

flower — flour

PAGE 21

Write the correct word under each picture.

1. __weigh__ weigh / way
2. __sun__ son / sun
3. __doe__ dough / doe
4. __flour__ flower / flour
5. __cheep__ cheap / cheep
6. __steak__ stake / steak
7. __eight__ ate / eight
8. __sail__ sale / sail
9. __male__ male / mail
10. __sew__ sew / so
11. __bear__ bare / bear
12. __sea__ sea / see
13. __pear__ pare / pear / pair
14. __pair__ pare / pear / pair
15. __pare__ pare / pear / pair

PAGE 22

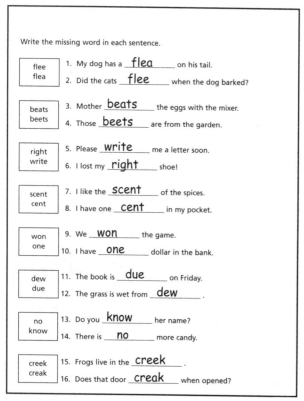

Write the missing word in each sentence.

flee / flea	1. My dog has a __flea__ on his tail.
	2. Did the cats __flee__ when the dog barked?
beats / beets	3. Mother __beats__ the eggs with the mixer.
	4. Those __beets__ are from the garden.
right / write	5. Please __write__ me a letter soon.
	6. I lost my __right__ shoe!
scent / cent	7. I like the __scent__ of the spices.
	8. I have one __cent__ in my pocket.
won / one	9. We __won__ the game.
	10. I have __one__ dollar in the bank.
dew / due	11. The book is __due__ on Friday.
	12. The grass is wet from __dew__.
no / know	13. Do you __know__ her name?
	14. There is __no__ more candy.
creek / creak	15. Frogs live in the __creek__.
	16. Does that door __creak__ when opened?

PAGE 23

Write the missing word on the line provided.

1. My __son__ Ted is six.
2. I __ate__ a hot dog.
3. __I__ lost my key.
4. Comb your __hair__.
5. I hurt my __right__ arm.
6. Pick a __flower__.
7. I went last __night__.
8. I __see__ a baby bird.
9. My dog eats __meat__.
10. Let's __sail__ the boat.

sun	son
ate	eight
eye	I
hair	hare
right	write
flour	flower
night	knight
see	sea
meat	meet
sale	sail

PAGE 24

Match the words that sound the same. Write the number beside the word it matches.

1. right	2. bear	3. dear	4. eight
5. cent	6. sea	7. I	8. flour
9. pear	10. so	11. blew	12. ring

7 eye	1 write	10 sew	9 pair
12 wring	3 deer	2 bare	8 flower
11 blue	6 see	4 ate	5 scent

PAGE 25

Context Clues are clues you can find in a sentence to help you figure out **what a word means**. Read the sentence:
The mouse felt **puny** standing next to the elephant.
Elephants are big and mice are small. That is a **clue** that can help you figure out that **puny** means **little**.

Choose a word from the word box to replace the **boldfaced** word in each sentence. Write it on the line provided.

shake	brave	smell	copy	~~little~~
strong	tease	choose	disappear	

1. The mouse felt **puny** standing next to the elephant.
   little

2. Sour milk can have a bad **odor**.
   smell

3. I get mad when big kids **taunt** my sister.
   tease

4. The people will **elect** a new president.
   choose

5. It was so cold I began to **quiver**.
   shake

6. These trees look **sturdy** enough to climb.
   strong

7. I saw the light in the distance **vanish**.
   disappear

8. My brother can **imitate** the sound of a bird.
   copy

9. The **courageous** knight fought the mean dragon.
   brave

PAGE 26

Choose a word from the word box to replace the **boldfaced** word in each sentence.

Let's exchange places.   Yes, let's Trade places.

| trade | smile | hit | shine | path |
| spin | move | burn | extra | dressed |

1. She can really **whack** the ball.   hit

2. The dancer began to **twirl**.   spin

3. I couldn't **budge** the heavy box.   move

4. The teacher said to **exchange** papers.   trade

5. The silly joke made him **grin**.   smile

6. A hot iron can **scorch** clothes.   burn

7. The **spare** tire is in the trunk.   extra

8. We followed the **trail** back to camp.   path

9. Waxing the car made is **gleam**.   shine

10. The king was **clad** in royal robes.   dressed

PAGE 27

Read this story about learning to skate. Then answer the questions.

Many times I had **longed** to be able to ice skate. Finally my big sister agreed to teach me.
I was filled with **glee** as I laced up my skates for the first time. I thought I would be **gliding** over the ice in minutes. Was I surprised when I stood up and fell right on the ice. It sure was **chilly**!
My sister helped me up and said, "Don't **fret**. After a few more **tumbles** you'll be skating like a star!"

1. Which **boldfaced** word in the story means:

   a. cold? chilly
   b. wished? longed
   c. joy? glee
   d. worry? fret
   e. moving? gliding
   f. falls? tumbles

2. Circle the best answer.

   a. The word **chilly** has to do with
      food   (temperature)   skates

   b. Which would most likely fill you with **glee**?
      being sick   (a surprise party)

   c. Which would you most likely **long** for?
      (a missing toy)   a broken pencil

   d. When would you be most likely to **fret**?
      (if you missed the school bus)   if you got a good grade

PAGE 28

Read each pair of words below. Choose the correct word for each sentence. Write the word on the line provided.

metal—shiny, hard material   **medal**—an award
through—in one side and out the other   **thorough**—complete
then—at that time   **than**—a comparison

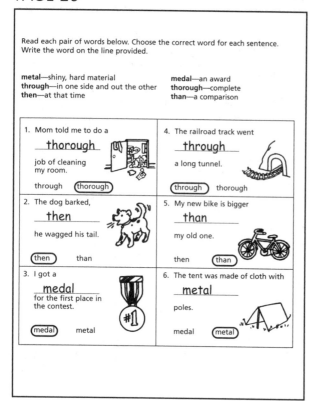

1. Mom told me to do a _**thorough**_ job of cleaning my room.
   through   (thorough)

2. The dog barked, _**then**_ he wagged his tail.
   (then)   than

3. I got a _**medal**_ for the first place in the contest.
   (medal)   metal

4. The railroad track went _**through**_ a long tunnel.
   (through)   thorough

5. My new bike is bigger _**than**_ my old one.
   then   (than)

6. The tent was made of cloth with _**metal**_ poles.
   medal   (metal)

PAGE 29

Read each pair of words below. Choose the correct word for each sentence. Write the word on the line provided.

quite—very   **quiet**—not noisy
loose—not tight   **lose**—misplace
guest—visitor   **guessed**—made a guess

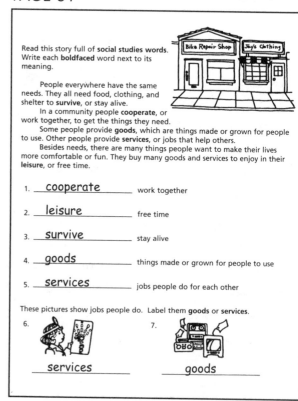

1. We had a _**guest**_ for dinner.
   (guest)   guessed

2. I promise not to _**lose**_ the note.
   loose   (lose)

3. The children kept _**quiet**_ during the fire drill.
   quite   (quiet)

4. The weather was _**quite**_ hot yesterday.
   (quite)   quiet

5. The children _**guessed**_ who was behind the mask.
   guest   guessed

6. My tooth was _**loose**_ so I didn't want to eat an apple.
   lose   (loose)

PAGE 30

Concept **words** are words that have to do with a certain **topic** or **idea**.
   One, subtract, and ten are all **math** words.
   Umpire, shortstop, base, and home run are all **baseball** words.

Read the words in the word box. Then find the correct word for each sentence. Write the word in the boxes.

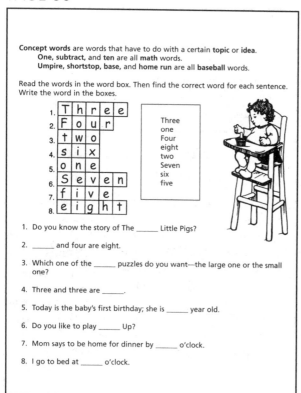

1. T h r e e
2. F o u r
3. t w o
4. s i x
5. o n e
6. S e v e n
7. f i v e
8. e i g h t

Word box: Three, one, Four, eight, two, Seven, six, five

1. Do you know the story of The _____ Little Pigs?

2. _____ and four are eight.

3. Which one of the _____ puzzles do you want—the large one or the small one?

4. Three and three are _____.

5. Today is the baby's first birthday; she is _____ year old.

6. Do you like to play _____ Up?

7. Mom says to be home for dinner by _____ o'clock.

8. I go to bed at _____ o'clock.

PAGE 31

Read this story full of **social studies words**. Write each **boldfaced** word next to its meaning.

People everywhere have the same needs. They all need food, clothing, and shelter to **survive**, or stay alive.
   In a community people **cooperate**, or work together, to get the things they need.
   Some people provide **goods**, which are things made or grown for people to use. Other people provide **services**, or jobs that help others.
   Besides needs, there are many things people want to make their lives more comfortable or fun. They buy many goods and services to enjoy their **leisure**, or free time.

1. _**cooperate**_ work together

2. _**leisure**_ free time

3. _**survive**_ stay alive

4. _**goods**_ things made or grown for people to use

5. _**services**_ jobs people do for each other

These pictures show jobs people do. Label them **goods** or **services**.

6. _**services**_

7. _**goods**_

PAGE 32

Read this story full of **science words**. Write each **boldfaced** word next to its meaning.

Scientists are looking for new **sources**, or places, to get energy. They are finding new ways to make, or **produce**, the power we will need in the future.

One kind of energy is **geothermal**. "Geo" means "earth" and "thermal" means "heat." Geothermal energy comes from heat that is already stored inside the earth.

Another kind of energy is **solar**. "Sol" means "sun." The sunlight is changed into energy we can use.

1. __geothermal__   heat from the earth

2. __solar__   from the sun

3. __produce__   to make

4. __sources__   places to get something

These pictures show kinds of energy. Label them **geothermal** or **solar**.

5. __solar__   6. __geothermal__

PAGE 33

Read the list of **science words** in the word box. Write each word in the correct list.

fishing pole	hummingbird
stinkbug	poodle
telephone	aquarium
television	redwood tree
mushroom	roller skates
laser beam	space shuttle
meteor	tadpole
toucan	crocodile
warthog	walkie-talkie

Living	Non-Living
stinkbug	fishing pole
mushroom	telephone
toucan	television
warthog	laser beam
hummingbird	meteor
poodle	aquarium
redwood tree	roller skates
tadpole	space shuttle
crocodile	walkie-talkie

PAGE 34

Read this passage full of **computer words**.

Computers may seem "smart" but they cannot think. The only thing they can do is follow a set of instructions called a **program** which must be written by a person. The computer **hardware** (machinery) and **software** (programs) work together.

For the computer to work, a person must enter **data**, or information, into the computer. This is called **input**. New data is entered by typing on a **keyboard** that has letters and symbols like a typewriter. Data may be stored on a **disk** which is used to record and save information.

Next, the computer "reads" the data and follows the instructions of the program. The program may tell it to organize the data, compare it to other data, or store it for later use. This is called data **processing**.

When the processing is complete, the computer can display the results either on the screen or printed on paper as a **printout**.

Find and write a **boldfaced** word from the story for each description.

1. __disk__   used to save and record information
2. __processing__   organizing, comparing, or storing data
3. __printout__   results printed on paper
4. __program__   set of instructions for a computer
5. __hardware__   computer machinery
6. __input__   entering data
7. __software__   computer programs
8. __keyboard__   where data is entered

PAGE 35

Sensory words are words that describe something you **smell, taste, touch, see** or **hear**.

Match the sense with the sensory word.

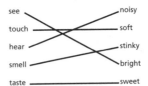

see — noisy
touch — soft
hear — stinky
smell — bright
taste — sweet

Write a sentence using each of the sensory words above.

1. _____
2. _____
3. _____
4. _____
5. _____

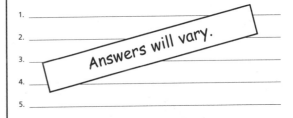

Answers will vary.

PAGE 36

Rewrite each sentence using two sensory words from the word box.

beautiful	sweet	boring
shiny	kind	tired
red	huge	stinky
fluffy	tiny	spotted
old	colorful	new
young	brown	broken
puppy	thrilling	exciting

1. I saw a butterfly.

_____

2. I have a dog.

_____

3. We saw a movie.

_____

4. This is my bike.

_____

5. My friend is.

_____

Answers will vary.

PAGE 37

Fill in each line with sensory words to complete the poem.

I see _____

_____

I hear _____

I taste _____

Answers will vary.

I smell _____

_____

I feel _____

_____

PAGE 38

Onomatopoeia is a word that **describes a sound**.
Clack, **boom**, and **splash** are all **onomatopoeia**.

Choose a word from the word box that describes the picture.

| sizzle | pop | moo | whir |
| hiss | whine | oink | howl |

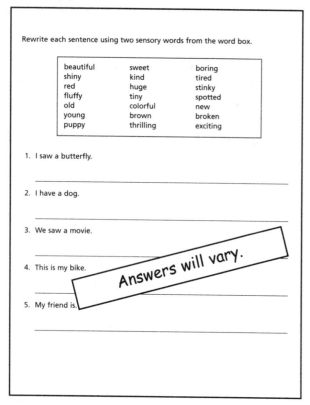

1. whir

2. sizzle

3. howl

4. hiss

5. pop

6. whine

7. moo

8. oink

PAGE 39

Read each onomatopoeia word in the word box. Write a sentence for each word describing how the noise was made.

clop	splash
pop	bang
squeak	buzz

1. _____

2. _____

3. _____

Answers will vary.

4. _____

5. _____

6. _____

PAGE 40

A **plural** word is **more than one** of a person, place, or thing.
The **plural** form of **nurse** is **nurses**.
The **plural** form of **city** is **cities**.
The **plural** form of **bag** is **bags**.

Add an **s** to the end of each word to make it plural.

1. rabbit ____rabbits____
2. duck ____ducks____
3. horse ____horses____
4. cow ____cows____
5. rooster ____roosters____
6. pig ____pigs____
7. llama ____llamas____
8. chick ____chicks____
9. goat ____goats____
10. hamster ____hamsters____

PAGE 41

Change each word to the plural form. Write the word on the line.
Change **f** to **v** and add **es**.
Change **y** to **i** and add **es**.

1. The ___leaves___ are pretty colors.
   leaf
2. We picked ___berries___ in the woods.
   berry
3. We saw a movie about ___wolves___ .
   wolf
4. The ___calves___ are in the barn.
   calf
5. There are two ___libraries___ in the city.
   library
6. Dad built ___shelves___ in the garage.
   shelf
7. It costs a dollar to ride the ___ponies___ .
   pony
8. The story is about seven tiny ___elves___ .
   elf
9. ___Fireflies___ are fun to watch at night.
   Firefly
10. Mother planted ___lilies___ in the yard.
    lily
11. The mother lion has three ___babies___ .
    baby
12. The police caught the ___thieves___ .
    thief

PAGE 42

Write each word in the plural form.
When a word ends in **ch**, **sh**, or **x**, add **es**.
Remember to change **y** to **i** and add **es**.

1. bunny ___bunnies___
2. story ___stories___
3. penny ___pennies___
4. city ___cities___
5. brush ___brushes___
6. size ___sizes___
7. match ___matches___
8. mailbox ___mailboxes___

PAGE 43

Write the plural form of each word next to its picture.
When a word ends in **vowel-o**, add **s**.
When a word ends in **consonant-o**, add **es**.

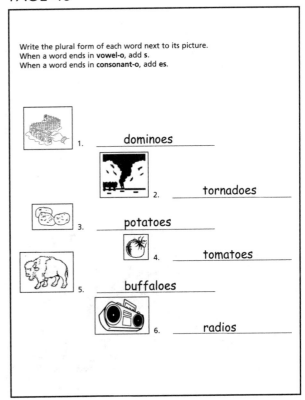

1. ___dominoes___
2. ___tornadoes___
3. ___potatoes___
4. ___tomatoes___
5. ___buffaloes___
6. ___radios___

PAGE 44

Some words have **irregular plurals**. Read the words in the word box. Write the plural form of the underlined word on the line to complete each sentence.

geese	women	cattle	oxen
men	moose	mice	children

1. The child __children__ rode the bus to school.

2. All those man __men__ are running in the race tomorrow.

3. Have you seen the goose __geese__ flying over head?

4. The team of ox __oxen__ pulled the plow.

5. These woman __women__ are all famous.

6. The mouse __mice__ in the garage have built a nest.

7. We saw moose __moose__ at the zoo.

8. Those cattle __cattle__ roam for miles on the ranch.

PAGE 45

A **suffix** is a part **added to the end** of a word. Suffixes change the meanings of words.
   In the word **packing**, ing is the **suffix**.
   In the word **wonderful**, ful is the **suffix**.

Add the suffix **ing** to a word from the word box to complete each sentence. Write the word on the line provided.

1. He is __asking__ questions.
2. We have been __packing__ clothes.
3. John has been __helping__ Father with the car.
4. Is Mother __cooking__ dinner?
5. Mark is __pulling__ weeds from the garden.
6. Is Nancy __locking__ all the doors?
7. Are you __going__ to the store?
8. Get your pole and let's go __fishing__ .
9. The children were __talking__ too loudly.
10. I have been __sleeping__ in bed all day.

PAGE 46

Add the suffix **ed** to a word from the word box to complete each sentence. Write the word on the line provided.

1. Mother __rocked__ the baby to sleep.
2. We __planted__ all the carrot seeds.
3. Bill and John __cracked__ open all the nuts.
4. That mule __kicked__ me!
5. Susan __climbed__ up the tree.
6. Our dog __barked__ all night long.
7. Father __parked__ our new car on the street.
8. Mary __painted__ the wall all blue.
9. It __rained__ cats and dogs today.

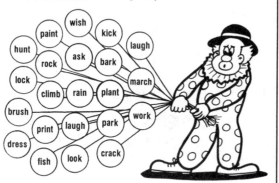

PAGE 47

Add the suffix **ful** to a word from the word box to complete each sentence. Write the word on the line provided.

1. The little puppy was very __playful__

2. Mark is __fearful__ of flying.

3. The cut on her finger was __painful__ .

4. Be __careful__ with that hot iron.

5. We are __hopeful__ we will get a new car.

6. Nancy is always so nice and __cheerful__

7. The peacock is a __colorful__ bird.

8. Ann is very __helpful__ to her mother.

9. A snake could be __harmful__ .

10. Mother had a very __restful__ nap.

11. They are __thankful__ the fire was not bad.

PAGE 48

Circle the suffix **less** or **ness** to complete each sentence.

1. The dark_____ scared us. less (ness)
2. I never had good grades in neat_____. less (ness)
3. The shot was pain_____ (less) ness
4. Oh, for good_____ sakes! less (ness)
5. The poor dog was home_____. (less) ness
6. The soft_____ of cotton feels good. less (ness)
7. This old toy is use_____ (less) ness
8. She loves the sweet_____ of oranges. less (ness)
9. Our new car is spot_____. (less) ness
10. His coat's thick_____ kept him warm. less (ness)
11. Don't be so care_____! (less) ness
12. Now I am tooth_____! (less) ness

PAGE 49

Add the suffix **ly** to the best word for each sentence. Write the word on the line provided.

1. Please don't talk so ___loudly___!
2. We must walk ___quickly___ or we'll be late.
3. That car ___nearly___ ran into us!
4. Daniel is a very ___friendly___ boy.
5. This traffic is moving too ___slowly___!
6. I can't see the boat ___clearly___ in this fog.
7. The baby is asleep. Play ___quietly___.
8. "What a ___lovely___ present," said Mother.
9. "You have ___hardly___ touched your dinner," said Dad.
10. The fireman ___bravely___ saved the little girl.
11. I will ___gladly___ do that for you.

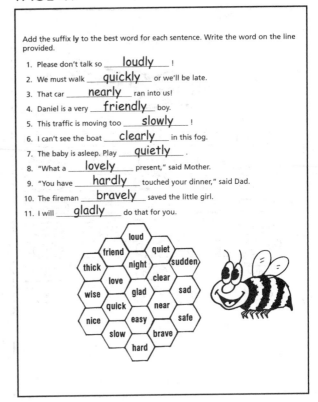

PAGE 50

sadly	friendless	sweetly
lifeless	cheerful	needless
nearly	toothless	careful

Find the word in the word box that matches each meaning below. Fill in the puzzle.

1. s w e e t l y
2. t o o t h l e s s
3. c h e e r f u l
4. n e e d l e s s
5. c a r e f u l
6. n e a r l y
7. s a d l y
8. l i f e l e s s
9. f r i e n d l e s s

1. with sweetness
2. no teeth
3. full of cheer
4. do not need
5. doing with care
6. almost
7. with sadness
8. without life
9. without friends

PAGE 51

A **prefix** is a part **added to the beginning** of a word. Prefixes change the meanings of words.

The **prefix** in **beside** is **be**.
The **prefix** in **impossible** is **im**.

Color the picture using the prefix code.

Prefix Code
be — yellow   a — red
mis — blue   sub — orange

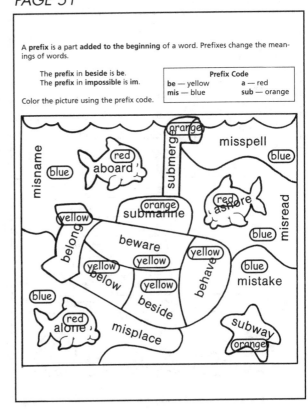

PAGE 52

Circle the words in each row that have the same prefix.

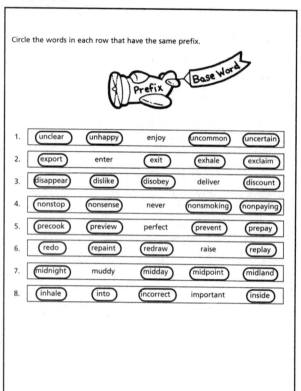

1. (unclear) (unhappy) enjoy (uncommon) (uncertain)
2. (export) enter (exit) (exhale) (exclaim)
3. (disappear) (dislike) (disobey) deliver (discount)
4. (nonstop) (nonsense) never (nonsmoking) (nonpaying)
5. (precook) (preview) perfect (prevent) (prepay)
6. (redo) (repaint) (redraw) raise (replay)
7. (midnight) muddy (midday) (midpoint) (midland)
8. (inhale) (into) (incorrect) important (inside)

PAGE 53

Read the prefix at the beginning of each row. Circle the prefix in each word in the row.

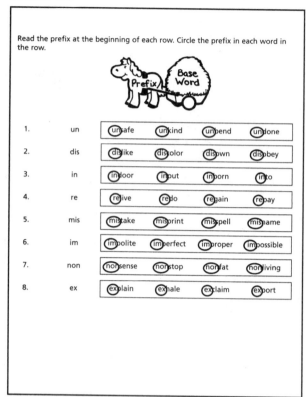

1. un | (un)safe (un)kind (un)bend (un)done
2. dis | (dis)like (dis)color (dis)own (dis)obey
3. in | (in)door (in)put (in)born (in)to
4. re | (re)live (re)do (re)gain (re)pay
5. mis | (mis)take (mis)print (mis)spell (mis)name
6. im | (im)polite (im)perfect (im)proper (im)possible
7. non | (non)sense (non)stop (non)fat (non)living
8. ex | (ex)plain (ex)hale (ex)claim (ex)port

PAGE 54

Read each word. Write the prefix in the **Prefix** column and the word without the prefix in the **Word** column.

	Prefix	Word
1. bicycle	bi	cycle
2. delay	de	lay
3. forearm	fore	arm
4. export	ex	port
5. adjust	ad	just
6. research	re	search
7. unclean	un	clean
8. misprint	mis	print
9. relive	re	live
10. telephone	tele	phone
11. uneven	un	even
12. repaint	re	paint

PAGE 55

Read each word. Write the prefix in the **Prefix** column and the word without the prefix in the **Word** column.

	Prefix	Word
1. aboard	a	board
2. replay	re	play
3. unkind	un	kind
4. inside	in	side
5. below	be	low
6. preschool	pre	school
7. mistake	mis	take
8. nonsense	non	sense
9. impress	im	press
10. dismiss	dis	miss

PAGE 56

Write each word under the correct heading. Circle the prefix or suffix in each word.

wind(y)	float(ing)	(sub)way	(re)write
fear(less)	(un)clear	hill(y)	(ex)cept
(in)side	(non)sense	kind(ness)	paint(ed)
beach(es)	hope(ful)	(re)name	(pre)cook

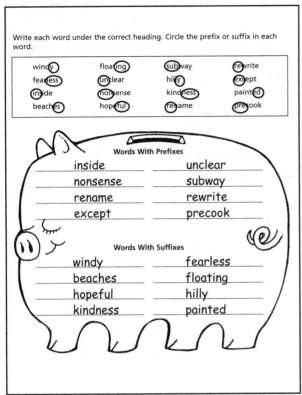

Words With Prefixes

inside	unclear
nonsense	subway
rename	rewrite
except	precook

Words With Suffixes

windy	fearless
beaches	floating
hopeful	hilly
kindness	painted

PAGE 57

A **root** or **base** word is the word that is left after you **take off a prefix or suffix**.
 A base word **can stand on its own**.
  Side is the base word of **inside**.
  Nerve is the base word of **nervous**.

A root word **cannot stand on its own**.
  Cept is the root word of **except**.
  Cess is the root word of **recess**.

Replace the underlined base word by adding a suffix to complete each sentence.

1. We go ice <u>skate</u> during the winter.   skating
2. Mom <u>bake</u> a cake for all of us.   baked
3. Who <u>clean</u> off the table?   cleaned
4. Are you <u>have</u> a good time?   having
5. Our dog has four <u>leg</u>.   legs
6. Mike went to two <u>party</u> this week.   parties

Circle the base word in each group.

1. preview   viewing   (view)
2. redo   did   (do)
3. liked   (like)   dislike
4. disagree   agreed   (agree)
5. called   (call)   calling
6. unrest   resting   (rest)

PAGE 58

Some prefixes are added to root or base words to tell how many. Use the prefixes in the word box to complete each sentence. Then write the definition in the blank beside each prefix.

uni- __1__	tri- __3__	deca- __10__
bi- __2__	quadr- __4__	

1. **Cycle** is a Greek word for circle or wheel. A two-wheeled vehicle is called a __bicycle__. Therefore, the **prefix bi-** means __2__.
 Young children ride a three-wheeled vehicle called a __tricycle__.
 The **prefix tri-** means __3__.
 A vehicle that has just one wheel is called a __unicycle__.
 Therefore, the **prefix uni-** means __1__.
2. **Ped** or **pod** are root words meaning foot. A **biped** is an animal with __2__ feet.
 The horse is a **quadruped**. It has __4__ feet.
 Our camera stand is called a **tripod**. It has __3__ feet.
3. A shape with ten sides is called a **decagon**. Therefore the **prefix deca-** means __10__.
 A **decapod** is an animal with __10__ legs and feet.
4. A **tricolor** is a flag with __3__ colors.
5. A **unicorn** has __1__ horn.
6. A school **uniform** is made in __1__ style for all students.
7. A **trimester** contains __3__ months.
8. A **quadruplet** is one of __4__ children born at the same time.
9. A **bilingual** person speaks __2__ languages.
10. A **triangle** has __3__ sides and __3__ angles.

PAGE 59

port	**to bring, to carry**
deport	to expel or send away from a country (from Latin *de-*, "away")
export	to send goods to another country (from Latin *ex-*, "out, out of")
import	to bring in from an outside source, especially from a foreign country (from Latin *in-*, "in")
portfolio	a flat case for carrying papers, manuscripts, drawings, or other documents (from Latin *folium*, "a leaf")

Fill in each blank with a word from the word box.

1. The artist kept her sketches in a leather __portfolio__.
2. People without official immigration papers can be __deport__ (ed) to their home countries.
3. The United States __import__ (s) oil from the Middle East.

Circle the root that means **to bring, to carry** in each word. Then write a brief definition on the line provided.

1. transportation
2. reporter
3. porter
4. supportive
5. portable

Answers will vary.

Vocabulary Answer Key

PAGE 60

scope	to look
kaleidoscope	a tube-shaped toy that one looks through to see a variety of changing colored patterns
microscope	an instrument for viewing objects too small to be seen by the naked eye
periscope	an instrument for viewing objects that are out of sight — used especially in submarines
scope	range of view or understanding; the space within which something exists, covers, or is limited to

Match each word with its use.

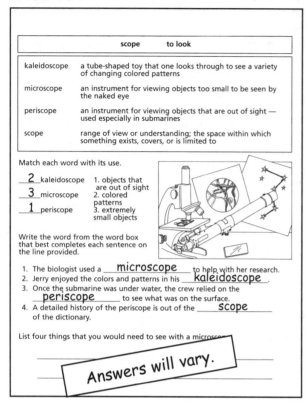

2 kaleidoscope
3 microscope
1 periscope

1. objects that are out of sight
2. colored patterns
3. extremely small objects

Write the word from the word box that best completes each sentence on the line provided.

1. The biologist used a ___microscope___ to help with her research.
2. Jerry enjoyed the colors and patterns in his ___kaleidoscope___.
3. Once the submarine was under water, the crew relied on the ___periscope___ to see what was on the surface.
4. A detailed history of the periscope is out of the ___scope___ of the dictionary.

List four things that you would need to see with a microscope.

___Answers will vary.___

PAGE 61

phon, phone	sound
megaphone	a funnel-shaped device for making sounds louder
microphone	an instrument that changes sound waves into electrical signals for transmission or amplification
phonetic	having to do with speech sounds
phonics	the rules of sound used in teaching reading and word pronunciation
xylophone	a percussion instrument made of tuned wooden bars struck with small hand-held hammers

Circle the root word that means **sound** in the following words.

1. micro**phone**
2. xylo**phone**
3. **phon**ics
4. mega**phon**e
5. **phon**etic

Write the word from the word box that best completes each sentence on the line provided.

1. Tyler learned to play the ___xylophone___ in music class.
2. Even with the ___megaphone___, it was hard to hear the cheerleaders over the crowd.
3. The singer used a headset ___microphone___ so her hands would be free for dancing.
4. We learned about the sounds of "c" in ___phonics___ class.

PAGE 62

-logy	the study of
archeology	the study of the life and culture of ancient people
meteorology	the study of weather
psychology	the study of the human mind and behavior
seismology	the study of earthquakes
zoology	the study of animals

Circle the root that means **the study of** in the following words.

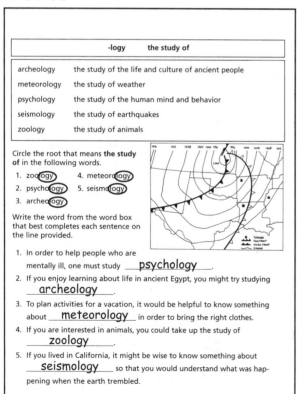

1. zo**ology**
2. psych**ology**
3. arche**ology**
4. meteor**ology**
5. seism**ology**

Write the word from the word box that best completes each sentence on the line provided.

1. In order to help people who are mentally ill, one must study ___psychology___.
2. If you enjoy learning about life in ancient Egypt, you might try studying ___archeology___.
3. To plan activities for a vacation, it would be helpful to know something about ___meteorology___ in order to bring the right clothes.
4. If you are interested in animals, you could take up the study of ___zoology___.
5. If you lived in California, it might be wise to know something about ___seismology___ so that you would understand what was happening when the earth trembled.

PAGE 63

Imported words are words used in English that come from **different languages**, such as Greek, Latin, French, or German.
Parka is a **Siberian** word.
Pamper is a **Dutch** word.

Write each word from the word box next to its definition.

vanilla (Spanish)	khaki (Hindi)
shampoo (Hindi)	crayon (French)
question (French)	cafeteria (Spanish)

1. A ___question___ means to ask or seek.
2. ___Shampoo___ is a soap used on hair.
3. A ___crayon___ is a piece of colored wax.
4. ___Khaki___ describes a color or a type of fabric.
5. A ___cafeteria___ is a place to eat lunch.
6. ___Vanilla___ is a flavoring used in desserts like ice cream and cookies.

Now write sentences using two of the words from above.

1.
2. ___Answers will vary.___

PAGE 64

Use the French words from the word box to complete the sentences.

> chef: someone who cooks
> buffet: many different foods on one table
> beret: a small hat
> catalogue: magazine of things for sale
> budget: a list setting aside money for bills, food, and other things
> ballet: a type of dance

1. My older sister wears a __beret__ when it is cold out.

2. I got this new __catalogue__ of video games in the mail.

3. Some of the football players are taking __ballet__ to become more graceful.

4. There are fried rice, sweet and sour chicken, and egg rolls on the __buffet__.

5. The __chef__ at this restaurant used to work with a very famous cook.

6. How much money did we __budget__ for the birthday gift?

PAGE 65

Read each sentence. Match the Arabic and Spanish words to their definitions.

> At sunset the sky was pink, **crimson**, and orange.
> The **asphalt** in the parking lot was very hot.
> Dad got a blue **brocade** sofa for the living room.
> The workers filled the truck with its **cargo** of fresh vegetables.
> The **bronco** tried to throw off its rider.
> Mom got a new **amber** ring for her birthday.

__a__ 1. a stone made of fossilized tree sap
__f__ 2. a rich fabric used in curtains or furniture
__b__ 3. a deep red color
__e__ 4. a type of horse
__d__ 5. suitcases, boxes, or other things a plane or truck may carry
__c__ 6. another word for black top or pavement

a. amber (Arabic)
b. crimson (Arabic)
c. asphalt (Arabic)
d. cargo (Spanish)
e. bronco (Spanish)
f. brocade (Spanish)

PAGE 66

Read the definitions of each word. Write a sentence using each word on the lines provided.

1. chocolate (Aztec)   a substance made from the cocoa plant used to make candy

2. clan (Italian)   family group

3. mango (Malaysian) a sweet, tro~~

4. ty~~

Answers will vary.

5. waffle (Dutch)   a hot breakfast food made in an iron that shapes the batter

6. jazz (African)   an American type of music

PAGE 67

Complete each phrase with an imported food word from the word box.

> bread (Old English)   shrimp (German)
> pizza (Latin)   mushroom (French)
> broccoli (Italian)   omelet (French)
> ketchup (Chinese)   vegetable (Latin)

1. Wheat, white, rye, cinnamon-raisin __bread__

2. Grows in the woods and tastes great on pizza __mushroom__

3. Beans, cauliflower, lettuce, peppers are all types of __vegetables__.

4. Made of eggs and filled with cheese and vegetables __omelet__

5. Comes from the Latin word for "pound" because that's what you do with the dough __pizza__

6. A tomato-flavored sauce to put on your burgers and fries __ketchup__

7. A green vegetable that looks like cauliflower __broccoli__

8. Take off the tails of these shellfish before you eat __shrimp__.

PAGE 68

An **abbreviation** is the **shortened** version of a word.

Read the words and their abbreviations in the word box.

Sunday—Sun.	January—Jan.
Monday—Mon.	February—Feb.
Tuesday—Tues.	March—Mar.
Wednesday—Wed.	April—Apr.
Thursday—Thurs.	August—Aug.
Friday—Fri.	September—Sept.
Saturday—Sat.	October—Oct.
	November—Nov.
	December—Dec.

Unscramble the abbreviations for the days of the week.

1. tsa   Sat.
2. nus   Sun.
3. onm   Mon.
4. edw   Wed.
5. sute   Tues.
6. rif   Fri.
7. rstuh   Thurs.

Unscramble the abbreviations for the months of the year.

1. bef   Feb.
2. mra   Mar.
3. ced   Dec.
4. tco   Oct.
5. rap   Apr.
6. vno   Nov.

PAGE 69

Write the letter of the abbreviation next to the word it matches.

street—St.	boulevard—Blvd.
yard—yd.	miles per hour—mph
foot—ft.	highway—hwy
mount—Mt.	apartment—apt.
avenue—Ave.	road—Rd.

d	1.	boulevard	a. mph
b	2.	street	b. St.
i	3.	highway	c. yd.
a	4.	miles per hour	d. Blvd.
g	5.	road	e. Ave.
e	6.	avenue	f. ft.
j	7.	apartment	g. Rd.
h	8.	mount	h. Mt.
f	9.	foot	i. hwy
c	10.	yard	j. apt.

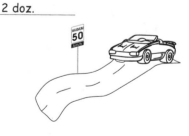

PAGE 70

Rewrite Emilio's birthday invitation using abbreviations. Rewrite all the numbers as numerals.

What:	Emilio's Tenth Birthday Party
When:	Friday, March Seventeenth at Three of the clock
Where:	Twenty-seven Oakstream Avenue

What:	Emilio's 10th Birthday Party
When:	Fri., Mar. 17th at 3 o'clock
Where:	27 Oakstream Ave.

PAGE 71

Rewrite each measurement using abbreviations.

1. 7 pounds   7 lb.
2. 5 ounces   5 oz.
3. 3 feet   3 ft.
4. 6 yards   6 yd.
5. 11 inches   11 in.
6. 2 centimeters   2 cm
7. 35 miles per hour   35 mph
8. 2 dozen   2 doz.

pounds:	lb.
miles per hour:	mph
ounces:	oz.
yards:	yd.
feet:	ft.
dozen:	doz.
centimeters:	cm
inches:	in.

PAGE 72

Write the day of the week and the date of each calendar event without abbreviations on the lines provided.

Jan.						
Sun.	Mon.	Tue.	Wed.	Thurs.	Fri.	Sat.
13	14 Evan's Birthday!	15 soccer 4 pm	16	17 dentist appt. 5:30 pm	18 Evan's Birthday Party 7 pm	19 Girl Scout mtg. 2 pm

Oct.						
Sun.	Mon.	Tue.	Wed.	Thurs.	Fri.	Sat.
20	21	22 piano lessons	23 soccer 4 pm	24	25	26 piano recital 6 pm
27	28 soccer 4 pm	29	30	31 Mom's Birthday!		

1. Monday, January 14
2. Tuesday, January 15
3. Thursday, January 17
4. Friday, January 18
5. Saturday, January 19
6. Tuesday, October 22
7. Wednesday, October 23
8. Saturday, October 26
9. Monday, October 28
10. Thursday, October 31

PAGE 73

A **compound word** is **made of two words** than can stand alone. **Cupcake** is a **compound word**.

Match a word from the bottom of the page with a word from the side of the page to make a compound word. Write the words on the lines provided.

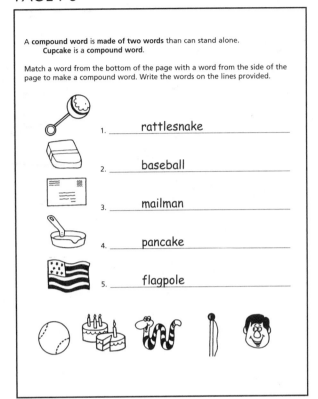

1. rattlesnake
2. baseball
3. mailman
4. pancake
5. flagpole

PAGE 74

Make a compound word from two words. Write the compound word.

1. flag + pole — flagpole
2. base + ball — baseball
3. dog + house — doghouse
4. butter + fly — butterfly
5. hair + brush — hairbrush
6. lady + bug — ladybug
7. bare + foot — barefoot
8. shoe + lace — shoelace
9. play + pen — playpen
10. cup + cake — cupcake

PAGE 75

Write the two words that make up each compound word.

1. blueberry — blue berry
2. popcorn — pop corn
3. football — foot ball
4. downstairs — down stairs
5. sidewalk — side walk
6. beehive — bee hive
7. raincoat — rain coat
8. snowstorm — snow storm
9. outside — out side
10. cowboy — cow boy

PAGE 76

Make crazy compound words by mixing up the compound words in the word box to make new ones. Write the word on the line and then draw a picture. The first one is done for you.

goldfish	mailbox	cheeseburger
eggshell	broomstick	treetop
hairbrush	junkyard	popcorn
snowman	seaweed	dishpan

goldfish + broomstick

1. __broomfish__

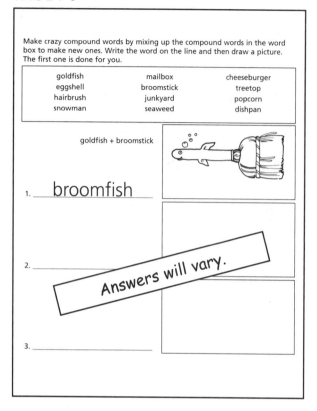

2. _____

Answers will vary.

3. _____

PAGE 77

Make more crazy compounds! Use the compound words in the box below.

horseshoe	bedroom	rattlesnake
farmhouse	butterfly	moonlight
football	bathtub	scarecrow
arrowhead	starfish	spaceship

1. _____

2. _____

Answers will vary.

3. _____

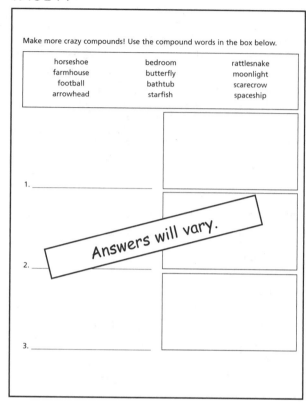

PAGE 78

Complete each sentence using a compound word from the word box.

fireflies	bathtub
scarecrow	cupcakes
campfire	watermelon
crosswalk	volleyball

1. This summer we spent many evenings around the __campfire__ .
2. We caught __fireflies__ in the dusk.
3. Mom and I baked __cupcakes__ for the bake sale.
4. Would you like some more __watermelon__ ?
5. Look both ways before using the __crosswalk__ .
6. Can you play __volleyball__ after school today?
7. We made a __scarecrow__ to frighten away the birds that were eating the garden.
8. Be careful not to slip when stepping out of the __bathtub__ .

PAGE 79

A **contraction** combines two words using an **apostrophe**. Not all of the letters in both words are written.
   We're is the contraction of **we are**; **I'll** is the contraction of **I will**.

Write two words from the word box for each contraction.

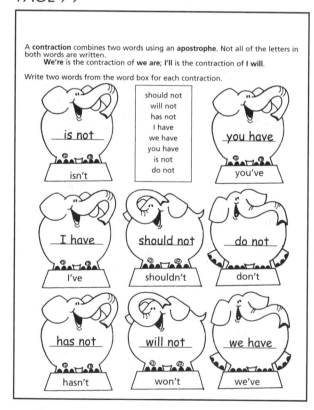

should not
will not
has not
I have
we have
you have
is not
do not

is not — isn't

you have — you've

I have — I've

should not — shouldn't

do not — don't

has not — hasn't

will not — won't

we have — we've

PAGE 80

Write the contraction from the word box in the space provided.

		Word Box
he's he is	I'm I am	he's won't don't didn't I'm we'll they're I've we're they'll
we'll We will	they're they are	
they'll they will	didn't did not	
we're we are	I've I have	

PAGE 81

Write a contraction of the two words in parentheses.

1. __I'll__ be home soon.
   (I will)

2. Jan __won't__ play.
   (will not)

3. We __aren't__ ready.
   (are not)

4. That __isn't__ my hat.
   (is not)

5. I think __she'll__ cry.
   (she will)

6. Tod __didn't__ find the cat.
   (did not)

7. __You'll__ like that book.
   (You will)

8. Hurry or __we'll__ be late.
   (we will)

9. Kim __doesn't__ live here.
   (does not)

10. __They'll__ ring the bell.
    (They will)

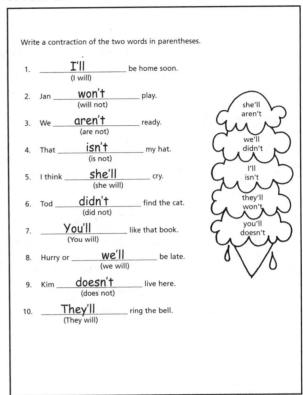

she'll / aren't
we'll / didn't
I'll / isn't
they'll / won't
you'll / doesn't

PAGE 82

Circle the missing words that complete each sentence. Then write the contraction of those words on the line provided.

1. We __weren't__ expecting a big crowd.
   did not / (were not)
2. Next time __I'll__ come early!
   (I will) / I am
3. We __haven't__ seen this movie.
   do not / (have not)
4. I know __you'll__ like it.
   (you will) / he is
5. This movie __isn't__ for adults.
   can not / (is not)
6. This line __hasn't__ moved.
   (has not) / we are
7. I __wouldn't__ want to be last in line!
   is not / (would not)
8. __They'll__ open soon.
   I am / (they will)
9. I __didn't__ bring my bubble gum.
   do not / (did not)
10. __Don't__ worry, we will get seats.
    Could not / (Do not)
11. Look, __they're__ selling tickets now.
    we were / (they are)
12. Ouch, __you're__ standing on my toe!
    (you are) / I am

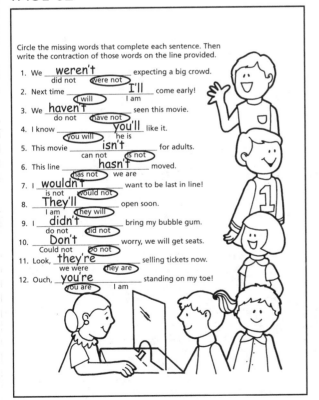

PAGE 83

Write the contractions.

do + not = __don't__	I + will = __I'll__
it + is = __it's__	will + not = __won't__
could + not = __couldn't__	they + are = __they're__
we + are = __we're__	she + is = __she's__
we + will = __we'll__	does + not = __doesn't__
who + is = __who's__	has + not = __hasn't__
you + are = __you're__	I + am = __I'm__
should + not = __shouldn't__	

Test-taking Practice is designed to prepare you to use the Vocabulary Skills you've been practicing in the first part of this book on a standardized test.

The first part of the Test-taking Practice is just for Vocabulary Skills. You'll answer questions that test your knowledge of synonyms, Antonyms, Homonyms, and Context Clues.

The second part of the Test-taking Practice is Reading Comprehension. On these pages, you will read a passage and then answer questions about it. The better your understanding of Vocabulary Skills, such as Context Clues, Concept Words, and Root and Base Words, the better you will do on Reading Comprehension, which indirectly tests these skills.

How to Use Test-Taking Practice

Getting Started:
- Read the directions carefully.
- Do the sample items.

Practice:
- Complete the Practice items.
- Continue working until you reach a Stop sign at the bottom of the page.

Sometime during school you may take a standardized achievement test. These tests check to see what you and the rest of your class have learned. they can help you see what your strengths and weaknesses are.

Taking a test can be stressful, but it doesn't have to be! The key is to prepare yourself, whether you are taking an achievement test or a weekly quiz. Here are some tips that can help you prepare for and do your best on any kind of test.

Before the test:
- Find a comfortable, quiet spot to study that is free of distractions.
- Get organized before you start to study: collect all the books, papers, notes, and pencils or pens you will need before you sit down.
- Study a little bit at a time, no more than 30 minutes a day. If you can, choose the same time each day to study in your quiet place. This is good practice for sitting and concentrating for the actual test.
- Give yourself frequent 5-minute breaks if you plan to study for longer than a half hour. Stand up, stretch out, and get a drink or snack (nothing too messy!)
- Try making a study sheet with all the information you think will be on the test. Have a parent, brother, sister, or friend quiz you by asking questions from the sheet.

On the day of the test:
- Get a good night's sleep before the test.
- Plan to eat a light breakfast and lunch so that you won't get drowsy during the test. Too much food can make you sleepy.
- Wear comfortable clothes that won't distract you during the test. If you have long hair, plan to pull it back away from your face so it won't distract you.
- Don't worry if you are a little nervous when you take a test. This is a natural feeling and may even help you stay alert.
- Take advantage of any breaks you have. Stand up and stretch, and get a drink of water or visit the bathroom if you have the time.

During the test:

Be careful

- Listen carefully to all the directions before you begin.

- Read all directions carefully.

- Sometimes the letters for the answer choices change for each question. Make sure the space you fill in matches the answer you think is correct.

- Read the question and all the answer choices. Once you have decided on the correct answer, ask yourself: "Does this really answer the question?"

Manage your time wisely

- Take the time to understand each question before you answer.

- Eliminate the answer choices that don't make sense.

- Try out answer choices in the question to see if they make sense.

- Skim through written passages and then read the questions. Refer back to the story to answer the questions. You don't have to reread the passage for each question.

- Look for key words in the question and the answer choices. They will help you find the correct answer.

- Sometimes the correct answer is not given. Mark "none" if this is the case.

- Skip difficult questions. Circle them and come back to them when you are finished with the easier questions.

- If there is still time when you have finished, go through the test again and check your answers.

Be confident

- Stay with your first answer. Change it only if you are certain another choice is better.

- Don't worry if you don't know an answer. Take your best guess if you are unsure of the answer, then move on to the next question.

- Be certain of what the question is asking before you answer. Try restating a question if you don't understand it the way it is written.

Examples

Directions: Read each item. Find the word that means the same or almost the same as the underlined word.

A costly ticket

ⓐ distant   ⓒ expensive

ⓑ ordinary   ⓓ winning

B I felt clumsy when I went skiing.

ⓕ tired

ⓖ graceful

ⓗ frightened

ⓙ awkward

 If you aren't sure of the answer, replace the underlined word with each answer choice and say the phrase to yourself.

Practice

1 search beneath

ⓐ beside   ⓒ above

ⓑ below   ⓓ along

2 free the animal

ⓕ release   ⓗ attract

ⓖ harm   ⓙ search

3 sometimes injure

ⓐ help   ⓒ miss

ⓑ carry   ⓓ hurt

4 view the scene

ⓕ leave   ⓗ observe

ⓖ enjoy   ⓙ purchase

5 Ellen's coat was ruined.

ⓐ cleaned

ⓑ repaired

ⓒ destroyed

ⓓ lost

6 The dry leaves were brittle.

ⓕ noisy

ⓖ damp

ⓗ colorful

ⓙ fragile

7 What do you do with stale bread?

ⓐ fresh

ⓑ old

ⓒ warm

ⓓ toasted

Examples   **Directions:** Read each item. Find the word or words that mean the same or almost the same as the boldface or underlined word.

A Bore a hole

- ⓐ stand beside
- ⓑ fall in
- ⓒ fill
- ⓓ drill

B A coat is like a —

- ⓕ hat
- ⓖ shoe
- ⓗ sweater
- ⓙ jacket

Stay with your first answer choice. Change it only if you are sure another answer is better.

Practice

1 A beautiful **meadow**

- ⓐ grassy field
- ⓑ dense forest
- ⓒ desert
- ⓓ swamp

2 Climb the **tower**

- ⓕ high hill
- ⓖ cliff
- ⓗ ladder
- ⓙ tall building

3 **Scatter** the seed

- ⓐ collect
- ⓑ bury deeply
- ⓒ throw around
- ⓓ harvest

4 To be **worried** is to be —

- ⓕ friendly
- ⓖ concerned
- ⓗ lost
- ⓙ injured

5 **A bucket is like a —**

- ⓐ box
- ⓑ net
- ⓒ pail
- ⓓ bag

6 To **pledge** is to —

- ⓕ sing
- ⓖ shout
- ⓗ promise
- ⓙ argue

7 **A trail is like a —**

- ⓐ path
- ⓑ forest
- ⓒ mountain
- ⓓ valley

Examples   Directions: Read each item. Choose the word that means the opposite of the underlined word.

A Caitlin will toss the ball first. Ⓐ hit Ⓑ catch Ⓒ throw Ⓓ find	**B buy some** Ⓕ none Ⓗ that Ⓖ several Ⓙ cheap

 Remember, you are looking for the answer that means the **opposite** of the underlined word.

Practice

1   Stony was pleased with his score.

Ⓐ happy

Ⓑ unsure

Ⓒ annoyed

Ⓓ satisfied

2   I stretched my sweater.

Ⓕ lost

Ⓖ washed

Ⓗ found

Ⓙ shrank

3   The train ride was jerky.

Ⓐ long

Ⓑ enjoyable

Ⓒ bumpy

Ⓓ smooth

4   work slowly

Ⓕ rapidly   Ⓗ kindly

Ⓖ harshly   Ⓙ soon

5   recent newspaper

Ⓐ delivered   Ⓒ old

Ⓑ thick   Ⓓ expensive

6   was furious

Ⓕ angry   Ⓗ curious

Ⓖ calm   Ⓙ uncertain

7   except Randy

Ⓐ like   Ⓒ including

Ⓑ with   Ⓓ despite

STOP

Examples

Directions: For items A and 1-3, read the two sentences with the blanks. Choose the word that fits both sentences. For items B and 4-5, find the answer in which the underlined word is used the same as in the sentence in the box.

A We looked in both _____ .

What do the _____ say?

- Ⓐ paths
- Ⓑ directions
- Ⓒ words
- Ⓓ boxes

B | The park is crowded today. |

In which sentence does the word **park** mean the same thing as in the sentence above?

- Ⓕ Where did you park the car?
- Ⓖ You will learn to park soon.
- Ⓗ The children played in the park.
- Ⓙ Park beside the supermarket.

 **Watch out! Only one answer is correct in both sentences or matches the meaning of the sentence in the box.**

Practice

1 Rosa paid a library _____ .

The carpenter did a _____ job.

- Ⓐ fee
- Ⓑ good
- Ⓒ fine
- Ⓓ great

2 Let's take a _____ now.

Did Randy _____ his skateboard?

- Ⓕ rest
- Ⓖ lose
- Ⓗ find
- Ⓙ break

3 Loren got a _____ for her work.

Be sure to _____ the dog's water.

- Ⓐ fee
- Ⓑ check
- Ⓒ fill
- Ⓓ reward

4 | Shara hurt her hand yesterday. |

In which sentence does the word **hand** mean the same thing as in the sentence above?

- Ⓕ Please hand me that bowl.
- Ⓖ The crowd gave the player a hand.
- Ⓗ On one hand, they did their best.
- Ⓙ Put your hand under the bag.

5 | In general, it was a good play. |

In which sentence does the word **general** mean the same thing as in the sentence above?

- Ⓐ He made a general comment about the food.
- Ⓑ The general will arrive soon.
- Ⓒ The small town had a general store.
- Ⓓ Lucy's mother is a general.

Examples   Directions: For items A and 1-3, read the paragraph or sentence. Find the word below that fits best in the blanks. For items B and 4-6, read the sentence with the underlined word. Find the word below that means the same or almost the same as the underlined word.

A   The children helped their parents _____ the family car. They used the garden hose for water.

   Ⓐ buy   © wash

   Ⓑ repair   Ⓓ sell

B   Many people visited the <u>famous</u> museum in our town. <u>Famous</u> means —

   Ⓕ large   Ⓗ science

   Ⓖ well-known   Ⓙ old-fashioned

 **Tips**   Use the meaning of the sentence to decide which answer choice is correct.

Practice

1   The test was _____ , but I did well.

Find the word that means the test was not easy.

   Ⓐ silent   © short

   Ⓑ difficult   Ⓓ simple

The rain ___(2)___ against the window. The thunder boomed and the ___(3)___ flashed.

2 Ⓕ attended   Ⓗ wet

   Ⓖ gushed   Ⓙ pounded

3 Ⓐ storm   © lightning

   Ⓑ weather   Ⓓ wind

4   The _____ cabin withstood the storm.

Which word means the cabin was strong?

   Ⓕ sturdy   Ⓗ cozy

   Ⓖ weak   Ⓙ huge

5   Are you <u>allowed</u> to go with us? <u>Allowed</u> means —

   Ⓐ happy   © permitted

   Ⓑ excited   Ⓓ ready

6   A safety <u>zone</u> surrounded the chemical plant. <u>Zone</u> means —

   Ⓕ fence   Ⓗ lake

   Ⓖ road   Ⓙ area

STOP

Examples   **Directions:** Read the phrase with the underlined word. Find the word below that means the same or almost the same as the underlined word.

E1 rely on her

Ⓐ breathe   Ⓒ depend

Ⓑ watch   Ⓓ stand

E2 accept a job

Ⓕ take   Ⓗ seek

Ⓖ reject   Ⓙ realize

1 sunshine is likely

Ⓐ enjoyable   Ⓒ impossible

Ⓑ rare   Ⓓ probable

2 cancel an order

Ⓕ stop   Ⓗ make

Ⓖ give   Ⓙ extend

3 happen frequently

Ⓐ quickly   Ⓒ occasionally

Ⓑ often   Ⓓ now

4 How can we attach this?

Ⓕ separate

Ⓖ connect

Ⓗ repair

Ⓙ examine

5 The house on the lake was lovely.

Ⓐ run-down

Ⓑ lonely

Ⓒ small

Ⓓ charming

6 Rare coins

Ⓕ cheap

Ⓖ beautiful

Ⓗ damaged

Ⓙ unusual

7 Inspect the food

Ⓐ freeze

Ⓑ carry

Ⓒ check carefully

Ⓓ cook well

8 A bundle is a —

Ⓕ friend   Ⓗ newspaper

Ⓖ mistake   Ⓙ package

9 To soar is to —

Ⓐ fly high   Ⓒ run around

Ⓑ sink quickly   Ⓓ follow closely

GO

Spectrum Vocabulary Grade 3

Directions: For numbers 10-14, read the phrase with the underlined word. Find the word below that means the opposite of the underlined word.

10 Those fish are very <u>colorful</u>.

    Ⓕ bright

    Ⓖ large

    Ⓗ strange

    Ⓙ dull

11 People <u>often</u> visit this beach.

    Ⓐ frequently

    Ⓑ rarely

    Ⓒ usually

    Ⓓ happily

12 The path to the lake is <u>straight</u> for about a mile.

    Ⓕ narrow

    Ⓖ wide

    Ⓗ crooked

    Ⓙ dangerous

13 feeling <u>excited</u>

    Ⓐ frightened   Ⓒ calm

    Ⓑ angry   Ⓓ nervous

14 <u>either</u> road

    Ⓕ neither   Ⓗ broad

    Ⓖ that   Ⓙ which

Directions: For numbers 15-16, find the word that fits in both sentences. For 17 and 18, find the answer in which the underlined word is used the same as in the sentence in the box.

15 Is _____ meat better for you?

    Don't _____ against the paint.

    Ⓐ fresh

    Ⓑ lean

    Ⓒ fall

    Ⓓ cheap

16 She got water from the _____ .

    Are you feeling _____ ?

    Ⓕ well

    Ⓖ bottle

    Ⓗ sick

    Ⓙ hungry

17 | Remember to <u>sign</u> your name. |

In which sentence does the word <u>sign</u> mean the same thing as in the sentence above?

    Ⓐ The <u>sign</u> blew down in the storm.

    Ⓑ Robins are a sure <u>sign</u> of spring.

    Ⓒ A small <u>sign</u> showed the way to the inn.

    Ⓓ Did you <u>sign</u> the form yet?

18 | How long will the storm <u>last</u>? |

In which sentence does the word <u>last</u> mean the same thing as in the sentence above?

    Ⓕ The movie will <u>last</u> until nine o'clock.

    Ⓖ Is this the <u>last</u> orange?

    Ⓗ The <u>last</u> part of the story is the best.

    Ⓙ Rudy moved here <u>last</u> year.   GO ▷

Directions: For items 19-28, read the sentences, then find the answer that fits best in the blank in the sentence or means the same as an underlined word.

19 Jasmine wanted to _____ the offer.

Find the word that means Jasmine wanted to think about the offer.

Ⓐ exceed   Ⓒ consider

Ⓑ dismiss   Ⓓ align

20 Thick beams _____ the roof.

Which word means the beams held the roof up?

Ⓕ supported   Ⓗ formed

Ⓖ weighed   Ⓙ aligned

21 The horse <u>approached</u> the fence. **Approached means —**

Ⓐ retreated   Ⓒ jumped over

Ⓑ came near   Ⓓ beyond

22 Do you <u>recall</u> who said that? **Recall means —**

Ⓕ replace   Ⓗ forget

Ⓖ dislike   Ⓙ remember

The __(23)__ of the country went on strike. They wanted the __(24)__ to treat them more fairly.

23 Ⓐ citizens   Ⓒ enemies

     Ⓑ voices   Ⓓ creatures

24 Ⓕ friend   Ⓗ ruler

     Ⓖ manager   Ⓙ register

T.J.'s family took a __(25)__ vacation. It was a __(26)__ trip that lasted a month and included a raft trip down the Colorado River.

25 Ⓐ minor   Ⓒ single

     Ⓑ plain   Ⓓ lengthy

26 Ⓕ certain   Ⓗ refunded

     Ⓖ wonderful   Ⓙ profitable

The price of shoes was __(27)__ because of a holiday sale. Marnie __(28)__ to buy tennis and running shoes.

27 Ⓐ increased   Ⓒ reduced

     Ⓑ unchanged   Ⓓ lost

28 Ⓕ decided   Ⓗ loaded

     Ⓖ avoided   Ⓙ rested

STOP

Examples

Directions: For items E1 and 1-9, read the phrase with the underlined word. Find the word that means the same or almost the same. For item E2, mark the answer that is the opposite of the underlined word. For item E3, find the word that best fits in both sentences.

E1 a huge rock

- ⓐ heavy
- ⓒ large
- ⓑ long
- ⓓ small

E2 borrow a pen

- ⓕ steal
- ⓗ lose
- ⓖ lend
- ⓙ find

E3 Do you _____ oranges?

Jim has a bicycle just _____ mine.

- ⓐ enjoy
- ⓑ about
- ⓒ squeeze
- ⓓ like

1 nasty weather

- ⓐ bad
- ⓒ normal
- ⓑ pleasant
- ⓓ acceptable

2 give commands

- ⓕ presents
- ⓗ changes
- ⓖ statements
- ⓙ orders

3 stay home

- ⓐ allow
- ⓒ respond
- ⓑ remain
- ⓓ leave

4 Her business is reliable.

- ⓕ dependable
- ⓖ successful
- ⓗ crowded
- ⓙ new

5 Are you certain about that?

- ⓐ happy
- ⓑ unsure
- ⓒ sure
- ⓓ sad

6 a cautious person

- ⓕ annoying
- ⓖ friendly
- ⓗ careful
- ⓙ healthy

7 to display a picture

- ⓐ paint
- ⓑ show
- ⓒ buy
- ⓓ sell

8 To be frail is to be —

- ⓕ weak
- ⓗ lost
- ⓖ strong
- ⓙ confused

9 To discard is to —

- ⓐ find
- ⓒ lose
- ⓑ trip over
- ⓓ throw away

STOP

Directions: For items 10-14, read the phrase with the underlined word. Find the word that means the opposite of the underlined word.

10 That trail might be <u>dangerous</u>.

    Ⓕ expensive

    Ⓖ enjoyable

    Ⓗ foolish

    Ⓙ safe

11 The group stayed <u>together</u> at the zoo.

    Ⓐ close

    Ⓑ far away

    Ⓒ apart

    Ⓓ with one another

12 The story about the family of bears made Ted <u>smile</u>.

    Ⓕ frown

    Ⓖ grin

    Ⓗ feel good

    Ⓙ feel amused

13 a cool <u>evening</u>

    Ⓐ drink   Ⓒ morning

    Ⓑ friend   Ⓓ product

14 <u>allow</u> a visit

    Ⓕ permit   Ⓗ conduct

    Ⓖ make   Ⓙ forbid

Directions: For numbers 15-16, find the word that fits in both sentences. For numbers 17-18, find the answer in which the underlined word is used the same as in the sentence in the box.

15 The swim _____ took place on Saturday morning at nine.

    Where did you _____ Sandra?

    Ⓐ meet

    Ⓑ find

    Ⓒ see

    Ⓓ match

16 Can you _____ in the ocean?

    Our _____ led the parade.

    Ⓕ swim

    Ⓖ band

    Ⓗ dive

    Ⓙ float

17 | **My <u>back</u> was sore after the game.** |

In which sentence does the word back mean the same thing as in the sentence above?

    Ⓐ Come <u>back</u> when you have finished.

    Ⓑ The dog is in <u>back</u> of the house.

    Ⓒ The pack on her <u>back</u> was heavy.

    Ⓓ The light in the <u>back</u> room is on.

18 | **How much did that <u>stamp</u> cost?** |

In which sentence does the word stamp mean the same thing as in the sentence above?

    Ⓕ <u>Stamp</u> your name on this form.

    Ⓖ This machine can <u>stamp</u> metal.

    Ⓗ A horse will often <u>stamp</u> its feet.

    Ⓙ There's no <u>stamp</u> on the envelope.

GO ▷

Directions: Read the sentences with the blanks. Choose the answer that fits best in the sentence or means the same as the underlined word.

19 We can all _____ the hall.

Find the word that means to make the hall beautiful.

Ⓐ visit   Ⓒ decorate

Ⓑ replace   Ⓓ attend

20 That light is too _____ for reading.

Which word means the light wasn't very bright?

Ⓕ dim   Ⓗ harsh

Ⓖ high   Ⓙ shallow

21 The picnic will have to be <u>delayed</u>. **Delayed means —**

Ⓐ started   Ⓒ planned

Ⓑ postponed   Ⓓ enjoyed

22 Did Brenda <u>reply</u> to your question? **Reply means —**

Ⓕ accept   Ⓗ startle

Ⓖ harness   Ⓙ answer

The dinner you served was ___**(23)**___ . We are grateful you remembered us. We'll ___**(24)**___ you to our house soon.

23 Ⓐ extended   Ⓒ delicious

Ⓑ realized   Ⓓ famous

24 Ⓕ invite   Ⓗ enjoy

Ⓖ accept   Ⓙ frequent

The manager was ___**(25)**___ with what the workers did. They finished on time and also saved a great deal of money for the ___**(26)**___ .

25 Ⓐ disappointed   Ⓒ busy

Ⓑ happy   Ⓓ confusing

26 Ⓕ company   Ⓗ reasons

Ⓖ benefit   Ⓙ acceptance

Be sure to ___**(27)**___ Clark Street. There's been an accident and traffic is ___**(28)**___ than usual.

27 Ⓐ travel   Ⓒ wait

Ⓑ standard   Ⓓ avoid

28 Ⓕ almost   Ⓗ moving

Ⓖ heavier   Ⓙ nearby

STOP

Examples   **Directions:** Read each item. Choose the answer you think is correct. Mark the space for your answer.

Yesterday morning, the governor signed the bill that will set aside five million dollars to improve state parks and hire school students to work in the parks during the summer.	**A This sentence would most likely be found in a —** Ⓐ biography. Ⓑ newspaper article. Ⓒ fairy tale. Ⓓ mystery.

 If a question seems confusing, try restating it to yourself in simpler terms.

Practice

1 Arnold is reading a story called "The Dream of Space Travel". Which of these sentences would most likely be at the very end of the story?

Ⓐ The dream has not come true, but it might in the near future.

Ⓑ Before the first plane was invented, people dreamed of space travel.

Ⓒ Rockets were invented by the Chinese almost 1000 years ago.

Ⓓ Stories of travel through the heavens are told in many cultures.

2 Which of these would most likely be found in a mystery story?

Ⓕ The President lives in Washington.

Ⓖ Bears eat many different foods.

Ⓗ Dolores opened the door slowly, but no one was there.

Ⓙ Before you can fix a leaky roof, you must find the leak.

3 A student is reading this story about the West.

The wagon train stopped for the night. Nan and Marty unhitched the horses and tied them to a nearby tree. The horses had fresh grass to eat and cold water to drink from a spring.

Which sentence is most likely to come next?

Ⓐ It was morning, and there was much to do before they could start out.

Ⓑ The first horses were brought to America by Spanish explorers.

Ⓒ The cottonwood tree made a strange shadow in the moonlight.

Ⓓ The two children hurried back to the wagon to help prepare dinner.

Examples Directions: Read each passage. Choose the best answer for each question that follows the passage.

"Have you seen my shoes?" "No. Didn't you leave them on the porch because they were muddy?" "I guess I did. I'll look there now. Don't leave without me."	**A These people are probably —** Ⓐ coming home Ⓑ resting Ⓒ arguing Ⓓ going out

 **Skim the story and then read the questions. Refer back to the story to answer the questions.**

Practice

"Do you hear something, Magda?"

"It sounds like a cat. Where could the noise be coming from?"

Magda and Mr. Howard went outside and looked to see what the noise was. They couldn't find anything. They looked under the car and behind the trash cans.

"Let's go back in, Magda. We can look around later if we hear the sound again."

"I want to look under the bush. Then I'll come in."

Magda crawled way under the bush beside the house. It was dark and she couldn't see very well. Just then, something furry crawled up against her face. Magda almost jumped out of her skin! It was a kitten, and it started licking her.

"Dad! Dad! Remember when you said I could have a kitten? I think my kitten just found me."

1 A bush is a kind of plant. Find another word that is a kind of plant.

Ⓐ rock   Ⓑ tree   Ⓒ garden

2 What caused Magda to "almost jump out of her skin"?

Ⓕ She heard something under the bush.

Ⓖ She wanted a kitten.

Ⓗ Something furry crawled up against her.

GO

"Mom, there's nothing to do. I'm bored."

"Why, Reggie, how can that be? We live in one of the biggest cities in the world. There are a million things for you to do. Why don't you walk down to the park?"

"That's really boring. Can I go over to Alida's? Aunt Millie said it's okay."

"That's a good idea. But go right over to the apartment. Don't stop in the video arcade like you usually do. I'll call Aunt Millie in about twenty minutes to check up on you."

Reggie grabbed his coat and hat and ran out the door and down the steps. He waited for the light to change, looked both ways, and crossed the street. There was always a lot of traffic on the street outside his apartment building, and he didn't want to get hit by a car.

He ran into the park and followed the path that went by the lake. Alida and her family lived on the other side of the park. Their apartment was almost a mile away, and he didn't want to waste time and worry his mother.

As Reggie passed the lake, he saw the strangest thing. A crowd of people was gathered around watching pirates row an old-fashioned boat on the lake!

Although he knew he should go right over to Alida's apartment, Reggie couldn't resist joining the crowd of people by the lake. When he got closer, he saw lots of lights, some cameras, and some people shouting orders at the pirates. It was very exciting, especially when the pirates got into a sword fight. None of them got hurt, of course, but one of them fell into the lake. Everyone got a good laugh at that.

After about ten minutes, Reggie suddenly remembered what he was supposed to be doing. He turned away from the crowd and started running down the path. If he hurried, he would still get to Alida's apartment before his mother called.

GO

3   Where do you think Reggie lives?

Ⓐ   On a quiet street

Ⓑ   Near a river

Ⓒ   On a busy street

Ⓓ   Near the ocean

6   About how long does it usually take to get to Alida's apartment?

Ⓕ   Less than twenty minutes

Ⓖ   More than twenty minutes

Ⓗ   About five minutes

Ⓙ   About thirty minutes

4   Which of these statements is probably true about Reggie?

Ⓕ   He never does what his mother says.

Ⓖ   His sister's name is Alida.

Ⓗ   He often jogs in the park.

Ⓙ   He likes to play video games.

7   What made Reggie remember what he was supposed to do?

Ⓐ   The sword fight

Ⓑ   Seeing someone fall in the lake

Ⓒ   Someone in the crowd

Ⓓ   The story doesn't say.

5   What made Reggie stop at the lake on his way to Alida's?

Ⓐ   Students who were practicing for a school play

Ⓑ   A crowd watching pirates

Ⓒ   Real pirates in the park

Ⓓ   Some people getting ready for Halloween

8   When he gets to Alida's house, Reggie will probably —

Ⓕ   make up a story explaining why he was late.

Ⓖ   explain what happened in the park.

Ⓗ   look for something to eat.

Ⓙ   ask Alida what happened in the park that day.

> Robbie got up early without anyone waking him. Today, he and the rest of the family were going fishing at Parker Lake. Robbie loved fishing, and Parker Lake had the best fishing around. They were going to rent a boat and spend the whole day on the lake. He was sure he would catch a big one.

A   How do you think Robbie feels?

Ⓐ   Worried

Ⓑ   Proud

Ⓒ   Excited

Ⓓ   Disappointed

 **Tips**   **Look for key words in the question and the answer choices. They will help you find the correct answer.**

Practice

Why should people drink milk?

Humans have probably been drinking milk for as long as they have been on earth. People who study the history of the world have found pictures from long, long ago that show people milking cows and using the milk for food.

Milk is the first food of babies. Animals that produce milk to feed their babies are called mammals. Their mother's milk is usually the best food for all young mammals.

The milk that people in America drink every day comes from cows, although many people prefer to drink the milk of goats. These two animals produce more milk than what their own babies need, and farmers collect the milk to sell it. In other countries, people also drink the milk of camels, horses, yaks, reindeer, sheep, and water buffaloes.

Milk is sometimes called the most nearly perfect food. It contains many of the things that humans need for healthy bodies, such as calcium, phosphorous, and protein. Milk also has several necessary vitamins and is easily digested by most humans. Another reason milk is such a good food is because some of its ingredients are found nowhere else in nature.

The one problem milk has is that it contains a lot of animal fat. This is good for young children, but not for adults. Foods with too much fat cause adults to have heart disease. Sometimes the fatty part of milk, the cream, is removed. This milk is called low-fat milk or skim milk. The cream that is removed from the milk is used to make ice cream and other foods. Milk is also used to make butter, cheese, and other dairy foods that people enjoy.

Besides being an important food, milk also provides chemicals that can be turned into other products. These chemicals are used to make paint, glue, cloth, and plastic.

GO >

1 **Which phrase from the story describes how good milk is?**

   Ⓐ ...the first food of babies...

   Ⓑ ...the most nearly perfect...

   Ⓒ ...easily digested by most humans...

   Ⓓ ...other dairy foods...

2 **Milk is used for all of these things except—**

   Ⓕ butter.

   Ⓖ fabric for clothing.

   Ⓗ paint for a house.

   Ⓙ automobile tires.

3 **Look at the picture on page 122. The picture shows the children —**

   Ⓐ drinking milk.

   Ⓑ eating something.

   Ⓒ waiting for someone.

   Ⓓ playing a game.

4 **Most of the milk that we drink comes from—**

   Ⓕ wild animals.

   Ⓖ big cities.

   Ⓗ yaks and water buffaloes.

   Ⓙ farm animals.

5 **Which of these would be best for an adult?**

   Ⓐ Ice cream

   Ⓑ Low-fat milk

   Ⓒ Butter

   Ⓓ Regular milk

6 **What is a word from the story that means "something made from other things"?**

   Ⓕ Ingredient

   Ⓖ Necessary

   Ⓗ Product

   Ⓙ Dairy

GO ▷

Graceful and Strong

Maria Tallchief was one of the most famous ballet dancers in the world. When she performed, the people in the audience loved to watch her dance. She was so graceful and so strong that she made the dancing look easy.

Born on an Osage Indian reservation in Oklahoma, Tallchief was given the name Betty Marie. Her mother thought the girl had special talents and tried to encourage them. When she was three, Tallchief began taking piano lessons. The next year, she started dance lessons even though most girls are not ready to start ballet until they are seven or eight years old. The young Tallchief did well in both piano and ballet.

Betty Marie's family moved to California so she and her sister could have more lessons. Betty Marie's teacher told her that a ballet dancer has to train harder than an athlete who plays football or baseball. Dance can be more challenging than any other sport, and Betty Marie worked as hard as she could.

Soon, Betty Marie's teachers told her she had to choose between ballet and piano. It was the only way she could develop her talent. She enjoyed both, but decided that she loved ballet more. When she was a teenager, she joined a Russian ballet group and changed her name. She thought Maria sounded more like a Russian name. She did not give up her Indian name, Tallchief.

Maria loved dancing, and people loved to watch her dance. She became famous all over the world. When Tallchief visited her home state of Oklahoma, the Osage Indian tribe made her a princess and performed Indian dances in her honor.

Tallchief continued to travel and dance, but she did not like being away from her family, especially her child. She stopped dancing to stay at home with her daughter. Later, Maria Tallchief started a ballet school to help other talented youngsters develop their dance skills. She wanted other girls to love ballet as much as she did.

GO

7 Maria Tallchief's two talents in childhood were ___ and ___.

Ⓐ Singing and dancing.

Ⓑ Playing piano and singing.

Ⓒ Dancing and playing piano.

Ⓓ Acting and singing.

8 Which of these is an opinion in the story?

Ⓕ The Osage Indian reservation is in Oklahoma.

Ⓖ People loved to watch Maria Tallchief dance.

Ⓗ Maria Tallchief started a ballet school for young dancers.

Ⓙ Maria Tallchief changed her first name but would not change her last name.

9 You can tell from reading this selection that ballet dancers must be—

Ⓐ beautiful and very smart.

Ⓑ able to play the piano very well.

Ⓒ tall and have long hair.

Ⓓ strong and willing to work hard.

10 At different times in her life, Maria had to make hard choices. She gave up all of these things except one. What did she not give up?

Ⓕ Playing piano

Ⓖ Her family

Ⓗ Ballet

Ⓙ The name Betty Marie

11 Why did the Tallchief family move from Oklahoma to California?

Ⓐ To live with relatives

Ⓑ So Betty Marie's father could get a better job

Ⓒ To give Betty Marie a chance to change her name

Ⓓ So Betty Marie could have better ballet lessons

12 Betty Marie's teacher compares ballet to —

Ⓕ sports that are easy.

Ⓖ games that are fun.

Ⓗ playing a musical instrument.

Ⓙ sports that require hard work.

GO

An Elephant Grows Up

Sikar was a 7-year-old male elephant. He had lived happily with his mother, aunts, and cousins in their herd in Africa. Sikar ate leaves and grass. He was tall enough to reach tender leaves in the trees.

Sikar's family often traveled as far as fifty miles in a day. They walked to find food and water. Sikar loved to play games with the other elephant children. He liked to put his whole body in the water. The elephants took water in their trunks and sprayed themselves and each other. Then they used their trunks to cover themselves with dust. They didn't do it just to be dirty. The dust helped keep away insects. Sikar was as happy as a young elephant could be.

One day, his mother told him the herd was leaving, but Sikar could not go with them. He would have to stay or go off on his own. "But why, Mama?" cried Sikar. Big tears rolled down his dusty cheeks. His huge ears flapped. His wrinkled, gray face looked even more wrinkled. "I want to stay with you. I love you, Mama."

"I know, dear, but you are almost grown now. I have the other children to care for. You must go with the older males. Our herd has only females and young males. I will always love you, Sikar, but you must grow up now," Sikar's mother explained carefully.

Sikar sadly went to find the other male elephants. He saw two young males who had been in his herd last year. They looked for food together, ate, played in the water, and threw dirt on each other. They even fought a little, but only in play. It was fun not to have his mother watching and calling out to him to be careful. He was lonely at night, though.

Sikar gradually forgot his old herd. He had become a gentle giant, an African elephant who weighed six tons. One day, he passed the herd of mothers and young elephants and saw his mother. She was busy with her children, and he was busy looking for food. Sikar thought about her for a minute, but then went on his way. He enjoyed his new life, and now that he was old enough to want a family, he must find a mate of his own.

GO >

13 From this story, you can conclude that elephants —

   Ⓐ always stay with the same herd.

   Ⓑ stay away from the water.

   Ⓒ don't play with one another.

   Ⓓ are bothered by insects.

14 Why did Sikar not want to go with the male herd?

   Ⓕ He did not like those elephants.

   Ⓖ He did not want to leave his mother.

   Ⓗ The food they found was not as good.

   Ⓙ He was bigger than the other elephants.

15 Sikar became —

   Ⓐ too hungry for his first herd.

   Ⓑ separated by accident from his mother.

   Ⓒ an unfriendly elephant.

   Ⓓ too old for his first herd.

16 The boxes show some things that happened in the story.

Sikar's mother said he should leave.		Sikar wanted a family of his own.
1	2	3

Which of these belongs in box 2?

   Ⓕ Sikar was lost in the jungle.

   Ⓖ Sikar joined a new herd.

   Ⓗ Sikar went to live with his mother again.

   Ⓙ Sikar was found in the jungle.

17 This story was written to—

   Ⓐ tell about how elephants live.

   Ⓑ teach a lesson about mothers and children.

   Ⓒ explain how elephants find food.

   Ⓓ show how large elephants are.

18 By the end of the story, Sikar was —

   Ⓕ still sad about leaving his mother.

   Ⓖ afraid of the larger elephants.

   Ⓗ less interested in his mother.

   Ⓙ unhappy with his new life.

STOP

E1

The balloon pilot turned on the burner. There was a huge whooshing sound and the balloon began to fill with hot air. Soon it started to rise into the air. In about fifteen minutes, it would be full, and they could take off.

The balloon is being filled with —

Ⓐ helium.

Ⓑ cold air.

Ⓒ hot air.

Ⓓ burning gas.

The way people entertain themselves in America has certainly changed in recent years. It was only about a hundred years ago that reading, singing, dancing, and playing musical instruments were all people had to amuse themselves. Then along came radio, and people didn't have to amuse themselves at all. They could simply listen and someone else would entertain them.

Motion pictures were the next great form of entertainment, and people could see and hear actors performing on the "big screen" in theaters around the country. The "small screen," television, soon made its way into almost every home, and people didn't even have to leave their couch to enjoy themselves. Video games and computers are the latest forms of entertainment technology, and who knows what inventions will be in our living rooms tomorrow.

1 **This story is mostly about —**

Ⓐ entertainers.

Ⓑ television and radio.

Ⓒ forms of entertainment.

Ⓓ technology.

2 **Which of these came first?**

Ⓕ Computers

Ⓖ Motion pictures

Ⓗ Television

Ⓙ Radio

For Number 3, choose the best answer to the question.

3 The giant picked up the two children and said, "Gosh, you've been so nice to me. What can I do to thank you?"

This sentence would most likely be found in a —

Ⓐ fairy tale.

Ⓑ biography.

Ⓒ newspaper article.

Ⓓ mystery story.

GO

How did Lilia feel about visiting her grandmother?

Lilia tried hard to keep the tears from filling her large, brown eyes. She felt like a heavy lump was in her chest. School was out, and all her friends were happily planning swimming lessons and family vacations. Lilia's mother had just told her she would have to go far away to spend the summer at Grandmother's. Lilia loved Grandmother, but she would be lonely without her family and friends in the neighborhood.

Lilia's mother put her arms around Lilia and brushed back her long, dark hair. Mrs. McGill had been sick and needed a great deal of rest this summer. Grandmother would take good care of Lilia, and she would come home at the end of summer. Everything would be better then. Lilia sniffed and nodded. She knew her mother was right, but she was still sad.

On the day she arrived, Lilia tried to find something wrong at Grandmother's house, but she couldn't. It had flowers, trees, and a white fence. Grandmother baked bread and cooked the same kind of food that Lilia's mother made at home. Grandmother smiled and told her, "I'm so glad you've come, Lilia."

Grandmother showed Lilia her pet bird, Bitsy, and the dog, Charley. Bitsy chirped at her, and Charley brought his ball for Lilia to throw.

That afternoon, Lilia saw some children next door. She asked Grandmother about them. Grandmother said, "Oh, that's Sally and her brother, Sid. They are twins, and they are the same age as you. I know you'll get along and play together. Their mother and I have lots of things planned for the three of you."

Lilia smiled. She would miss her family and friends back home, but this might be a good summer after all!

GO

4 In the story, Lilia felt—

Ⓕ sad and then happy.

Ⓖ sad all through the story.

Ⓗ happy and then disappointed.

Ⓙ happy all through the story.

5 This story is written to show—

Ⓐ children have a hard time when their parents are sick.

Ⓑ things often work out better than you think at first.

Ⓒ a child can never be happy away from home for the summer.

Ⓓ grandmothers are not as much fun as mothers.

6 Lilia's grandmother had—

Ⓕ no children as neighbors.

Ⓖ a small house with no yard.

Ⓗ a swimming pool in her back yard.

Ⓙ a bird and a dog for pets.

7 Lilia was a girl who—

Ⓐ tried not to show her mother that she was sad.

Ⓑ did not get along with other children her own age.

Ⓒ was rude to her grandmother when she went to visit.

Ⓓ complained because she was unhappy going to her grandmother's.

8 Why did Lilia smile in the last paragraph?

Ⓕ She knew she would be spending the summer at her own home.

Ⓖ She didn't want Grandmother to see her cry.

Ⓗ She knew she would be happy being away from home.

Ⓙ She loved animals, and Grandmother had two pets.

9 Which words in the story show that Grandmother was trying to make things fun for Lilia?

Ⓐ ...Lilia saw some children next door...

Ⓑ She would miss her family and friends back home...

Ⓒ Their mother and I have lots of things planned...

Ⓓ ... this might be a good summer...

10 Which would be a good title for this story?

Ⓕ My Grandmother

Ⓖ A Surprising Summer

Ⓗ New Friends

Ⓙ Bitsy and Charley

GO

Lucy sat very still as the plane took off. She liked flying, but always felt a little funny when the plane took off and landed. This plane was smaller than any other she had ever been on, and she didn't know what it would be like.

The take-off was smooth, and in a few minutes, they were flying high above the ground. All around them, Lucy could see the ocean.

The plane headed south from Miami toward Key West. Lucy, her mother, and her two brothers were going there to visit her father. He was in the Coast Guard and was stationed in Key West.

Lucy looked out the window and saw a chain of islands. Her mother said they were the Florida Keys. A road and a series of bridges connected the islands. Key West was the last island in the chain.

"Mom, how come they are called keys?"

"It's from the Spanish word *cayo*, which means island or reef. The first European explorers here were from Spain."

The water below had lots of different colors. The deepest water was dark blue, and along the shore, it was very light. In between, there were many shades of blue. On this background of blue were lots of boats, some with sails and some with motors. As the boats moved across the surface, they left streaks of white in their wake.

Lucy heard the sound of the engines change and the plane started its descent. In a few minutes, she would see her father for the first time in weeks. It would also be the beginning of a vacation she would remember forever.

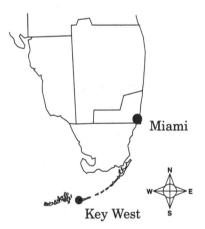

Miami

Key West

11 Which of these is true about Lucy?

Ⓐ She had never flown on a plane before.

Ⓑ She was afraid of flying.

Ⓒ She often flies on small planes.

Ⓓ She had never flown on a plane this small before.

12 When Lucy flies back to Miami, in which direction will she travel?

Ⓕ North

Ⓖ South

Ⓗ East

Ⓙ West

13 How did Lucy first know the plane was about to land?

Ⓐ She saw the airport.

Ⓑ The pilot turned the plane toward the airport.

Ⓒ The sound of the engines changed.

Ⓓ The pilot made an announcement over the intercom.

14 What can you conclude about the water around the Florida Keys?

Ⓕ Deeper water is lighter in color than shallow water.

Ⓖ Deeper water is darker in color than shallow water.

Ⓗ It seems to be very rough.

Ⓙ It seems to be very calm.

15 Why was Lucy going to Key West?

Ⓐ To visit her father

Ⓑ To visit her mother

Ⓒ To move there

Ⓓ To go to school there

16 What kinds of things do you think Lucy will do in Key West?

Ⓕ Climb mountains, ski, and go ice skating

Ⓖ Stay inside and watch television because it is cold

Ⓗ Swim, ride in a boat, and lie on the beach

Ⓙ Visit farms and ride on a tractor

E1

The cat was curled up in a tiny ball beside the fire. When she heard Martin walk into the room, she opened one eye first and then the other. Domino slowly stood up and stretched. She blinked twice and followed him toward the kitchen.

The cat was probably —

Ⓐ playing.

Ⓑ hunting.

Ⓒ purring.

Ⓓ sleeping.

The travelers found themselves in a forest of talking trees. Just then, all the trees began talking at once. They were so loud that it was impossible to understand what they were saying.

1 **Which sentence is most likely to come next in the story?**

Ⓐ Once upon a time a group of travelers started on a long journey.

Ⓑ No one knew where they were and they became frightened.

Ⓒ Suddenly, the biggest tree said, "Quiet, everyone!"

Ⓓ The outside of the trunk of a tree is called the bark.

What I remember most about that big old house in Iowa was the kitchen, a room that was always warm and always smelled wonderful.

2 **This sentence would most likely be found in —**

Ⓕ a newspaper article.

Ⓖ an autobiography.

Ⓗ a fairy tale.

Ⓙ a science book.

3 **Which of these would most likely be found in a newspaper article?**

Ⓐ "Now hold on there," said the sheriff, "we don't put up with things like that in this town."

Ⓑ It wasn't a star they were looking at, but a spaceship, and it was coming right at them.

Ⓒ Guido said good-bye to his family, picked up his bags, and joined the crowd walking toward the ship.

Ⓓ A recent report from the school board stated that there are more students in school than ever before.

4 **Sally is reading a book called *Home Gardening for Young People*. Which of these sentences would most likely be at the beginning of the book?**

Ⓕ After you have planted the seeds, you'll have to keep them watered so they don't dry out.

Ⓖ Few things are as rewarding as tending a garden.

Ⓗ Now comes the fun part, eating the vegetables you have raised.

Ⓙ The most difficult part of having a garden is making sure that weeds don't take over.

GO

Last Sunday, my dog Buddy started scratching his face. Pretty soon, it was red and sore. I was really worried.

"Mom, something is wrong with Buddy. Look at his face."

"This doesn't look very good, Lucas. Let's put some medicine on it and see what happens. If it doesn't get any better, we'll have to take him to the doctor."

I rubbed the medicine on Buddy's face and was very careful not to get it into his eyes. He didn't like it very much, but he held still for me.

The next day, he was even worse, so Dad stayed home from work, and he and I took Buddy to the veterinarian. The doctor examined Buddy and gave us some pills. We had to give them to Buddy three times a day. The doctor said it would be easiest if we mixed it into food or a treat. The doctor also gave us a special collar that would keep Buddy from scratching his face. When we put the collar on, Buddy looked like a clown, but I felt bad for him.

I gave Buddy his medicine every day just like the doctor said. For a day or two it didn't seem to help. Then Buddy stopped trying to scratch his face. Pretty soon, his face started to get better.

A week later, my Aunt Janelle and I took Buddy back to the doctor. He examined Buddy again and said he was okay. The veterinarian thought that Buddy had an allergy, kind of like when I start to sneeze when Dad cuts the lawn. He said we should keep an eye on Buddy to see if we could find out what he was allergic to. If we found out, we could avoid it in the future.

GO

5   How do you think Lucas felt at the end of the story?

Ⓐ Worried because Buddy had an allergy

Ⓑ Happy because Buddy had an allergy

Ⓒ Disappointed because the doctor couldn't fix the problem

Ⓓ Relieved because Buddy was getting better

6   Who is telling this story?

Ⓕ Lucas

Ⓖ Buddy

Ⓗ Aunt Janelle

Ⓙ The doctor

7   What made Buddy look like a clown?

Ⓐ Scratches on his nose

Ⓑ The medicine on his face

Ⓒ A special collar

Ⓓ The pills

8   We know that Lucas is a responsible person because he —

Ⓕ rode in the car to the doctor with Aunt Janelle.

Ⓖ gave Buddy his medicine every day.

Ⓗ tried to get to school on time.

Ⓙ felt bad because Lucas had to wear a funny collar.

9   A lesson you can learn from this story is to —

Ⓐ avoid cutting the grass when the wind is blowing.

Ⓑ keep dogs inside as much as possible.

Ⓒ avoid things to which you are allergic.

Ⓓ be careful when you put a new collar on a dog or cat.

GO ⟩

He Changed the World

"Chris. Christopher. Chris-to-pher! Come home for dinner!" Chris heard his mother's voice, and walked home slowly. He was watching a ship in the harbor near his home. The sailors were unloading wonderful things that had been brought from far away. There were mysterious bundles and smells that Chris did not recognize. The ship had just come from Asia. The sailors were sunburned and happy. They talked to the young boy on the dock.

When he reached his home, Christopher told his mother, "A ship just came in. It was wonderful. When I grow up, I want to be a sailor. I want to go places and see things."

The boy was Christopher Columbus. He lived in Genoa, Italy, a city by the sea. Genoa was one of the busiest seaports in the world when Chris was born in 1451. He did become a sailor when he was a teenager, and he did see the world.

In the 1400s, ships carried things from Asia to Italy and other places. They brought jewels, ivory, silks, and spices. The ships carried the goods part of the way, and then they had to be unloaded so camels and other animals could carry everything across land. Then the goods would be loaded on another ship to finish the trip.

Christopher Columbus thought he could find a way to go all the way to Asia by water. Many people in his time thought the earth was flat, but he thought it was round. He wanted to sail west to reach Asia. If Columbus could find a new, shorter route to Asia, he would become rich and famous.

Columbus was not poor, but he did not have the money to buy ships for such a trip. He couldn't find any money in his own country. He went to the king and queen of Spain, Ferdinand and Isabella. They first said no, but they changed their minds. They agreed to buy Columbus three ships and give him money to make his trip.

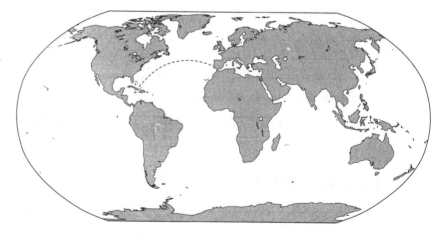

After being at sea for two difficult months and facing many dangers, Columbus saw land. He and his sailors thought they had arrived in Asia and were very excited. They had not found Asia, however. Instead, they had reached the New World, what we now call America. Columbus never got rich, but many others followed. He had changed the world forever.

10 **Why didn't Christopher Columbus sail in his own ships?**

   Ⓕ The king would not let him.

   Ⓖ He couldn't find any sailors for his ships.

   Ⓗ Only kings and queens could own ships.

   Ⓙ He didn't have enough money.

11 **This story was written to tell the reader—**

   Ⓐ how Columbus spent his fortune.

   Ⓑ about sailing ships in the 1400s.

   Ⓒ about ships going to Asia.

   Ⓓ how Columbus achieved his dream.

12 **What word in the story means "difficult to explain, strange, unusual"?**

   Ⓕ Mysterious

   Ⓖ Recognize

   Ⓗ Explorer

   Ⓙ Seaport

13 **Christopher became interested in sailing because —**

   Ⓐ his father was a sailor.

   Ⓑ he dreamed about an adventure.

   Ⓒ he lived by the sea.

   Ⓓ his family owned ships.

14 **What mistake did Christopher Columbus and his sailors make?**

   Ⓕ They sailed in a circle and landed in Europe.

   Ⓖ They found Asia instead of America.

   Ⓗ They found America instead of Asia.

   Ⓙ They had not really found land.

15 **Which of these does this story lead you to believe?**

   Ⓐ Columbus did not know about Asia when he left Spain.

   Ⓑ Columbus did not know about the New World when he left Spain.

   Ⓒ The king and queen made Columbus a rich man.

   Ⓓ Columbus knew the world was flat but tried anyway.

16 **Which of these is most like what happened in the story?**

   Ⓕ Bridgette was looking for her homework and found a ring she had lost a week ago.

   Ⓖ Andrew enjoys sailing and hopes to own a boat when he grows up.

   Ⓗ Kate and her family planned a vacation carefully and really enjoyed their trip to a national park.

   Ⓙ Jake surprised his sister by giving her a party on her birthday.

GO

Schedule for Camp Tonawanabee

Week of July 8 - 13

Eight and nine-year-old campers should check in at camp office between 12 noon and 5 P.M., July 7.

7:00 - 8:30	Wake up, breakfast, clean up	**1:30 - 2:30**	Ping-pong for 8-year-olds
8:30 - 9:30	Boys' swimming		Crafts for 9-year-olds
	Girls' basketball	**2:30 - 3:00**	Break
9:30 - 10:00	Break	**3:00 - 4:00**	Horseshoes
10:00 - 11:00	Boys' basketball	**4:00 - 5:00**	Hiking
	Girls' swimming	**5:00 - 6:30**	Dinner, rest
11:00 - 12:30	Lunch, rest	**6:30 - 7:30**	Softball or volleyball
12:30 - 1:30	Crafts for 8-year-olds	**7:30 - 8:30**	Movie or group singing
	Ping-pong for 9-year-olds	**8:30 - 9:00**	Cabin meetings, snacks
		9:00 - 9:30	Ready for bed, lights out

For more information, call Marissa Johnson at 903-555-1214.

Counselors for 8-year-olds:
Adam Sands, head counselor, boys;
Jack Smithey; Charlie Carlson.
Mary Jones, head counselor, girls;
Sue Martin; Ericka Stevens

Counselors for 9-year-olds:
Joe Johnson, head counselor, boys;
Cedric White; Aaron Lang.
Lisa Gomez, head counselor, girls;
Heather Case; Shalonda Moore

GO

17 **At what time do the boys have swimming?**

Ⓐ 8:00 - 9:00

Ⓑ 8:30 - 9:30

Ⓒ 10:00 - 11:00

Ⓓ 1:30 - 2:30

18 **Which of these activities is <u>not</u> in the morning?**

Ⓕ Swimming

Ⓖ Crafts

Ⓗ Breakfast

Ⓙ Basketball

19 **Sylvester is a 9-year-old boy. He started a braided leather key chain in crafts class on Tuesday. At what time on Wednesday will he go to crafts again to finish it?**

Ⓐ 11:30 - 12:30

Ⓑ 12:30 - 1:30

Ⓒ 1:30 - 2:30

Ⓓ 3:00 - 4:00

20 **What are the rest times for all campers?**

Ⓕ After lunch and after dinner

Ⓖ Before lunch and after dinner

Ⓗ Before lunch and before dinner

Ⓙ After lunch and before dinner

21 **Whom would you call for more information about the camp?**

Ⓐ Marissa Johnson

Ⓑ Joe Johnson

Ⓒ Mary Jones

Ⓓ Charlie Carlson

22 **Eight-year-old Toby and 9-year-old Tina are a brother and sister going to Camp Tonawanabee this summer. Which activity will they have together?**

Ⓕ Crafts

Ⓖ Ping-pong

Ⓗ Hiking

Ⓙ Swimming

23 **Who is the head counselor for 9-year-old girls?**

Ⓐ Joe Johnson

Ⓑ Mary Jones

Ⓒ Sue Martin

Ⓓ Lisa Gomez

24 **Which of these happens last?**

Ⓕ Basketball

Ⓖ Boy's swimming

Ⓗ Ping-pong

Ⓙ Softball

STOP

Page 107
A. C
B. J
1. B
2. F
3. D
4. H
5. C
6. J
7. B

Page 108
A. D
B. J
1. A
2. J
3. C
4. G
5. C
6. H
7. A

Page 109
A. B
B. F
1. C
2. J
3. D
4. F
5. C
6. G
7. C

Page 110
A. B
B. H
1. C
2. J
3. B
4. J
5. A

Page 111
A. C
B. G
1. B
2. J
3. C
4. F
5. C
6. J

Page 112
A. C
B. F
1. D
2. F
3. B
4. G
5. D
6. J
7. C
8. J
9. A

Page 113
10. J
11. B
12. H
13. C
14. F
15. B
16. F
17. D
18. F

Page 114
19. C
20. F
21. B
22. J
23. A
24. H
25. D
26. G
27. C
28. F

Page 115
E1. C
E2. G
E3. D
1. A
2. J
3. B
4. F
5. C
6. H
7. B
8. F
9. D

Page 116
10. J
11. C
12. F
13. C
14. J
15. A
16. J
17. C
18. J

Page 117
19. C
20. F
21. B
22. J
23. C
24. F
25. B
26. F
27. D
28. G

Page 118
A. B
1. A
2. H
3. D

Page 119
  A. D
  1. B
  2. H

Page 121
  3. C
  4. J
  5. B
  6. F
  7. D
  8. G

Page 122
  A. C

Page 123
  1. B
  2. J
  3. A
  4. J
  5. B
  6. H

Page 125
  7. C
  8. G
  9. D
  10. G
  11. D
  12. J

Page 127
  13. D
  14. G
  15. D
  16. G
  17. A
  18. H

Page 128
  E1. C
  1. C
  2. J
  3. A

Page 130
  4. F
  5. B
  6. J
  7. A
  8. H
  9. C
  10. G

Page 132
  11. D
  12. F
  13. C
  14. G
  15. A
  16. H

Page 133
  E1. D
  1. C
  2. G
  3. D
  4. G

Page 135
  5. D
  6. F
  7. C
  8. G
  9. C

Page 137
  10. J
  11. D
  12. F
  13. C
  14. H
  15. B
  16. F

Page 139
  17. B
  18. G
  19. C
  20. F
  21. A
  22. H
  23. D
  24. J

Notes

Notes

Notes